How To Conquer Clutter

by Stephanie Culp

WRITER'S DIGEST BOOKS
Cincinnati, Ohio

How to Conquer Clutter. Copyright © 1990 by Stephanie Culp. Printed and bound in the United States of America. All rights reserved. No part of this book may be reproduced in any form or by any electronic or mechanical means including information storage and retrieval systems without permission in writing from the publisher, except by a reviewer, who may quote brief passages in a review. Published by Writer's Digest Books, an imprint of F&W Publications, Inc., 4700 East Galbraith Road, Cincinnati, Ohio 45236. (800) 289-0963. Revised edition.

Other fine Writer's Digest Books are available from your local bookstore or direct from the publisher.

06   05   04   03   14   13   12   11

Library of Congress Cataloging-in-Publication Data

Culp, Stephanie.
  How to conquer clutter/Stephanie Culp.
     p.   cm.
  1. House cleaning.   I. Title.
TX324.C85   1989   89-32984
648—dc20   CIP
ISBN 0-89879-362-9

for
Sandra Tolman (Bryant)
gone, but not forgotten

Acknowledgments

Books are influenced by more than just the author, and this book is no exception. My clients have always been a source of inspiration as we work together to conquer their mountains of clutter. I have learned something from each and every one of them.

At Writer's Digest Books, thanks to Mert Ransdell, who made what could have been an annoying negotiating experience an efficient, satisfying one, and to Jo Hoff, whose enthusiasm, tact, and cheerfulness are always appreciated. Even Hugh Gildea, in accounting, responds promptly and with good humor to my questions. Writer's Digest Books is a good place to be.

Shu Yamamoto has my gratitude for his artistic talents, and when it comes to editors, there is nobody who can match the analytical, organizational, and creative talents of the editor on this book, Beth Franks. I'd like to work with Shu and Beth on all of my projects!

Book deadlines invariably lead to typewriter breakdowns, so special thanks go to my rescuers: Fred Gutkind, who repairs my typewriter; and Tom Driscoll, who always rushes over with a loaner at moment's notice.

Finally, thanks go to Jim (Ron) Reed, who provides (almost) daily love and support, and to Fritz, who comforted and amused me during the many hours I spent writing this book.

Table of Contents

Waging War on Clutter

3 Clutterbug's Excuse Almanac
5 Seven Clutter Warranties
6 Interior Design à la Clutter
10 The Cost of Clutter
  11 Clutter Quiz
16 It Could Always Be Worse
  22 Ten Commandments on Clutter
  24 Surviving a Mine Field of Clutter Traps
24 Developing Your Battle Plan
25 A Place for Everything
27 How to Use This Book

Clutter from A to Z

29 Addresses (see Business Cards, Phone Numbers)
29 Announcements
30 Antiques
30 Appliances
32 Art & Art Supplies
32 Baby Clothes
33 Bags
34 Balls
34 Baskets
35 Bathroom Clutter
36 Batteries
36 Books
37 Boxes
38 Brochures
40 Bulletin Boards
40 Business Cards
41 Calendars
42 Candles
43 Canning Supplies
43 Car Accessories & Supplies
44 Cards
45 Catalogs
48 Children

49 Cleaning Supplies
50 Clocks
52 Closets
54 Clothes
62 Collections
63 College Papers
64 Cosmetics
66 Craft Supplies
67 Desk
72 Dishes
74 Electrical Supplies
74 Exercise Equipment
75 Eyeglasses
75 Files & Filing Cabinets
83 Furniture
84 Gadgets
85 Games
86 Gardening Equipment & Supplies
86 Gifts
87 Handbags
89 Hardware
90 Hats
91 Heirlooms
93 Holiday Decorations
94 Husbands
96 Invitations (see Announcements)
96 Jewelry
98 Junk
99 Junk Drawer
100 Keys
101 Kitchen Utensils
102 Knickknacks

103 Lamps
103 Laundry
105 Linens
107 Love Letters
108 Lumber
108 Magazines
110 Mail
114 Makeup (see Bathroom Clutter, Cosmetics)
114 Maps
115 Memorabilia
116 *National Geographic*
116 Newspapers
117 Notes
118 Office Supplies
119 Packing Materials
120 Paint & Paintbrushes
122 Papers
130 Pens & Pencils
131 Pet Paraphernalia
132 Phone Numbers
133 Photographs
133 Plaques (see Souvenirs, Trophies)
133 Postcards
134 Posters
136 Pots & Pans
136 Purse (see Handbags)
136 Recipes
139 Rocks
139 Salt & Pepper Sets
140 School Papers (see College Papers, Children—Papers)
140 Sewing Supplies

141 Shoes & Boots

142 Shopping Bags

142 Socks & Stockings

144 Souvenirs

145 Spices

146 Sports Equipment

147 Stuffed Animals

148 Suitcases

149 Ties

150 Tools

151 Toys

153 Trays (see Pots & Pans)

153 Trophies

154 Uniforms

154 Vacuum Cleaner
     Attachments

155 Vases

155 Videotapes

156 Wallets

156 Wine

157 Wives

158 Clutterbusters to Live By

162 It's Your Turn: Answers to Commonly Asked Questions

166 Storage: Clutter Containers

178 Recycling Your Clutter Cast-Offs

180 Resource Helpline

Waging War on Clutter

CLUT•TER To fill with scattered or disordered things that restrict movement or efficiency; a crowded or jumbled mass or accumulation; disorder. Or, all that *stuff* you've got all over the place that everybody keeps telling you to get rid of.

Sooner or later, clutter invades nearly everyone's life. In a world that focuses increasingly on *things* that accumulate with startling ease, finding the time to enjoy, care for, store, and catalog all these objects and materials can be more and more difficult. For some, the clutter is confined to one area; for example, too many books or magazines and not enough time to read them, or a messy garage. For others, clutter starts as a small problem and, over time, becomes a very large and seemingly overwhelming situation. As they sink deeper and deeper into the chaos, excuses become almost traditional. Clutterbugs, as a general rule, seem to follow certain patterns as they edge toward clutter chaos. These are a few of your more basic clutter types:

The Stasher

The Stasher *stashes* everything. If there is a closet or cabinet door to hide things behind, the Stasher will open it and start stashing. The Stasher often stashes good things along with useless clutter; they drag home used books covered with mildew only to stash them with the good jewelry or antiques already in the cupboard. On the surface, the Stasher looks neat; but don't believe it for a minute! When the Stasher comes out of the closet, you'll find a pack rat, pure and simple.

The Spreader

Spreaders can be found anywhere, but are most obvious in an office setting. It is impossible for Spreaders to work on one piece of paper at a time. They are only happy if they can spread papers over every available surface. No matter how neat their desk looked when they started, everything is spread all over the place within five minutes of their arrival. Then they layer the spread by constantly adding to the mess without ever attempting to (gasp!) get rid of or put away any of the papers from the many layers. When anyone comments on the plethora of papers, the Spreader screeches, "Don't touch anything. I know *exactly* where everything is!" And the truth is , most of the time, they do. But it takes twenty minutes to unearth a piece of paper (they know *which* pile it's in, after all—it's just a matter of digging it out). Spreaders often claim to be overworked and underpaid. They are convinced that nobody else could handle the very important paperwork that falls under their domain. Most of the time, only about 20 percent of those papers have any value at all; the rest could be tossed or filed. And the remaining 20 percent could probably be handled by somebody else much more efficiently. Just ask any Spreader who has been fired for "not being able to handle the workload." Spreaders create work where there is none and never get to what really needs to be done. They're too busy spreading.

The Messie

The Messie makes little messes all over the place. For example, getting dressed in the morning is a mess, particularly since, when the Messie does the laundry, *that* turns into a mess with clean clothes in little piles everywhere. This necessitates a search for the pile with the clean underwear before actual dressing can begin. The Messie probably made a mess of his/her toys as a child. While the Stasher sometimes tries to pack as much as possible into a closet or cupboard, the Messie bypasses "packing" altogether. They opt instead to *toss* things into piles, which are inside and outside of closets and cupboards. They often have an apparently easygoing personality and act as if the messes aren't there (even as they add to the messes). When people survey the Messie's messes and exclaim, "What a mess!" the bewildered Messie cries, "What mess?"

The Procrastinator

Serious Procrastinators try very hard to procrastinate to the point where they will never have the time to deal with any of the clutter in their lives. These folks are often heavy-duty perfectionists as well. They put things off because they don't have time to do it perfectly. They don't do the filing because they don't have exactly the right labels for the file folders (the labels have to be ordered from Outer Podunk, so chances are they never will get those labels). So the filing turns into piles that turn into paper mountains. They don't clean out the garage because they need some shelving, which only they can install, and before they can install it, they need a super-fandangled tool (which, of course, is not at the local hardware store and never will be). So now the garage holds everything *but* the car. Procrastinators often run around in a tizzy doing absolutely nothing and getting totally exhausted in the process. Many Procrastinators are well-read. They read all the time. All of this reading material just adds to the general clutter, and the time it takes to read leaves very little time — if any — for getting organized and putting the accumulated clutter away. Procrastinators are very clever people. They put a great deal of time, thought, and energy into the act of procrastinating. If they put half as much time into getting organized, they could probably go into the business and be professional organizers.

The Pack Rat

Pack Rats are the ultimate hoarders. They keep everything and live in terror of the thought that something might actually get thrown away. Pack Rats live by their own code of logic regarding the actual value of the things that come into their lives. *Everything* has value to the Pack Rats. When Pack Rats run out of room to store their accumulation, they simply go out and purchase more room. They rent storage units or buy larger houses and as soon as they have done that, they very methodically fill them up. Pack Rats pack their stuff all over the place: in piles, boxes, and bags; in closets and cupboards; under the bed; on any available shelving; on tables and counters; behind the sofa; and in drawers all over the house. When those spaces fill up, they simply start stacking clutter against walls and on any other available floor space. If anyone dares to try to get rid of some of the Pack Rats' stash (say, for example, by tossing twenty-year-old newspapers), the Pack Rats head — fuming — straight to the garbage cans and pull everything back out that had been tossed. Then, regardless of the condition of the item, they drag it back into the house. This is when the Pack Rats start reaching the point of no return. Once this stacking-out-in-the-open and garbage-digging begins, it is only a matter of time before there is a system of narrow pathways through the house (which is otherwise piled high with their hoard of mostly useless clutter). Pack Rats who achieve this ominous clutter gridlock often need serious professional help.

Nearly everybody stashes, spreads, messes, procrastinates, or mindlessly hoards at one time or another. Regardless of your clutter condition—from spotty (a little clutter here and there) to sporty (cluttering is the thing you do best; you are a champion at cluttering and collecting)—nearly everybody, at one time or another, resorts to the Clutterbug's list of excuses to defend their clutter accumulation:

Clutterbug's Excuse Almanac

I can't get rid of that because . . .
- I might need it someday.
- There's an article I have to read in that (magazine or newspaper).
- It'll be worth money someday.
- It will come back in style if I wait long enough.
- It was a gift.
- I paid good money for it.
- As soon as I lose twenty pounds, I'll be able to wear it again.
- It's still perfectly good.
- It doesn't belong to me; it belongs to _____ (fill in the blank).
- I inherited it.
- It just needs to be fixed and it will be good as new.
- They don't make things like that anymore.
- I'm saving it for _____ (fill in the blank with some mythical day or event).
- It would cost a fortune to replace.
- It brings back memories.

Armed with any or all of the excuses found in the Almanac, the clutterbug handles clutter by saying, "I'll just put it over here *for now.*" Before you know it, "for now" turns into forever, and it becomes obvious that something must be done to regain control of the clutter.

This book will help you help yourself, whether your clutter problem is small or of magnificent proportions. It helps you decide what to get rid of and gives you storage ideas for what's left. Finally, it gives you lots of common sense advice and practical tips that will help you keep clutter under control in the future.

You can apply the clutter control techniques in this book to your home or office. If you have a home-based office, this book will help you maximize and organize the limited space you have available for all of your activities.

But first things first. Start by dealing with the excuses:

I might need it someday. This is like putting a bet down in Las Vegas. You *might* need it someday—then again you might not. How long have you been playing this hand? If you still haven't needed it, it's time to cash in your chips and quit this game.

There's an article I have to read in that. There's very little in life that you really *have* to do. Since you obviously *can't* do, see, taste, read, or have it all, perhaps you can start accepting that fact by letting go of some of those articles now.

It will be worth money someday. Yeah, but are you going to see the day? And while we're on the subject, how much is it *costing* you to store in the meantime?

It will come back in style if I wait long enough. Oh, puleaze! Even if it does come back in style, it will be in a slightly different cut and fabric, and you'll still look a little nerdy around the edges.

It was a gift. It's the thought that counts. So give it as a gift to someone else (like charity).

I paid good money for it. Whose fault is that? Just because you made one stupid mistake doesn't mean you should make another mistake by keeping the first mistake.

As soon as I lose twenty pounds, I'll be able to wear it again. By that time, this rag will be totally out of style.

It's still perfectly good. If it's still so dad-gummed good, how come you never use it?

It doesn't belong to me; it belongs to _____ . So call up _____ and tell them you are moving their stuff to outside storage and having the bill sent to them. This goes for your college-aged son's stuff as well as the load of stuff you promised to keep temporarily for the neighbor who moved last year. What are you, a moving and storage company?

I inherited it. Oh. Time to let someone else inherit it from you now, before you die.

It just needs to be fixed and it will be good as new. Send it out to be fixed.

They don't make things like that anymore. And for good reason: Nobody in their right mind would have one. Besides, it doesn't matter how well-made it is if you never use it.

I'm saving it for _____ (fill in that special day or event that may never happen — like that garage sale you've been talking about forever). It's been five years and that day still hasn't rolled around. What year do you anticipate this happening?

It would cost a fortune to replace. I know. Just think of all the money you'll save by dumping it and *not* replacing it with anything.

It brings back memories. Old tax returns bring back memories too. How many memories do you need, for Pete's sake?

So much for excuses. Or, put another way, so much for procrastinator poppycock. Now here are some Clutter Warranties:

Seven Clutter Warranties

1. Clutter is guaranteed to get ruined. Stack it, pack it, store it, and watch bugs and mice chew and do their duty on it. Rust, mildew, moths, sloppy packing, and storage guarantee the eventual ruination of your precious clutter.

2. **A cleaning warranty comes with clutter.** It's a sure bet that you'll waste lots of your spare time cleaning, dusting, washing, waxing, and scouring your clutter. And while you're busy cleaning the clutter, everybody else is at the beach.

3. **Expensive real estate is a guaranteed requirement for clutter.** You have to put clutter someplace, and whether it's a closet, filing cabinet, garage, or independent storage unit, storage is space and it costs money. Chances are, the square footage will appreciate in value faster than the clutter.

4. **Moving is guaranteed to be a financial and logistical royal pain in the neck.** Moving, whether it's down the street or across the country, will cost you dearly. You'll pay for every ounce of clutter that gets packed, and it will take you ten times longer than it should to make the move.

5. **A slow-down warranty accompanies all clutter.** Clutter will cramp your style and get in the way until productivity all but grinds to a painful halt. You can kiss progress (and probably that promotion you have your eye on) goodbye.

6. **Clutter guarantees loss.** It's impossible to keep track of things once clutter takes over. Losing things becomes standard operating procedure. You'll need to set aside time every day to frantically hunt for the most recently misplaced item that is buried somewhere in your clutter.

7. **Your image is guaranteed to take a beating with clutter around.** Clutterbugs, messies, and pack rats all look like incompetent boobs to the outside world. You won't appear even remotely in charge of your facilities to your boss or your mother-in-law.

Interior Design à la Clutter

Clutter is easily incorporated into any design scheme, be it Early Grandma or Fancy Smancy. Simply start piling clutter into the area and before you know it, you will have a design "statement" that, while not unique, definitely represents your personal style.

Although clutter can mix with any color and design scheme, there are specific areas that tend to attract clutter first. These areas are often closed off to public viewing. When the decorator makes a visit, it is generally wise to steer the artist firmly away from those areas. Of course, decorators tend to be an independent lot and, sooner or later, he or she will probably demand entry into the closed areas. When that happens, brace yourself. Clutter does not compute with most decorators, and when faced with something they cannot deal with, they often get hysterical. To avoid this future design problem, check these clutter areas for design conflict before you are faced with exposing them to a less than enthusiastic audience.

Attic

Although it's a safe bet that your decorator won't want to climb up into the attic, it is an area you need to look at. Some people can turn their attics into lofts; pack rats find that option inconceivable. A determined hoarder will somehow get all manner of things up into the attic, but when it comes time to get it down, that's different. Crying that the task is physically impossible, they throw up their hands and leave everything up there. It makes me think about natural disasters. For example, if there is a flood, you won't be able to retreat to the attic 'cause there won't be room for you. If there's an earthquake, all that clutter will fall on your head and kill you. Killed by clutter. What a way to go.

Basement

Some people turn their basement into a rec room and other people give it the wreck room effect. The clutter is boxed, bagged, and hauled down the stairs for indefinite storage. Next, people will start installing chutes so they can shove the stuff with one mighty heave to its final destination. When it's suggested that some of the clutter be removed from the basement, the pack rat perversely reverses the attic argument and hollers that the stuff is impossible to get up the stairs. Beam me up, Scotty.

Breezeway

I suspect breezeways were originally intended to allow breezes to flow through. Six-foot-high stacks of clutter obviously block those breezes. Since the breezeway is sort of inside but sort of outside, the mice and bugs sort of set up house among the clutter, where they contentedly munch away. Eventually they get a little too comfortable—protected as they are from the elements. They then brazenly eye the *inside of the house* where, they speculate, there is even more clutter and, therefore, food and housing for them and their little families. Oh boy.

Carport

The carport is somewhere between the design of the breezeway and the garage. Not entirely protected from the elements, some clutterbugs pause before stacking clutter in this location. After the pause, they do it anyway. When the rain gets to the boxes, the boxes collapse in a soggy mess, the contents squashed to smithereens. The clutterbug usually surveys the scene with dismay but, lacking a place to stack soggy boxes of clutter, does nothing, leaving the boxes (and the contents) to suffer this humiliating state for at least another year or two.

Closets

Closets, especially spare closets, provide a fertile hiding place for all manner of clutter, not the least of which is outgrown and outdated clothing. Shoving stuff in the closet *for now* becomes a way of life for pack rats. Eventually every closet is full, and the only solution for future life on this planet is to move to a house with more and bigger closets. This is an expensive solution to a clutter design problem, but your decorator will no doubt embrace it enthusiastically. After all, the decorator will then get to start *all over*, decorating yet another abode for you and your clutter. Clients like you keep decorators in business.

Garage

People often don't consider the design possibilities of their garage; clutterbugs are an exception. They eye the garage rabidly as they calculate how much clutter they can put there before the garage is full and they have to park the car on the street. Once that happens, they can get awfully creative. I knew a man who decided to get bids from a contractor on the cost of building a subterranean garage under his current garage, since clearing out the clutter was unthinkable as a potential solution to the problem. I always think of an Early American design for the garage because it really is the Final Frontier for clutter.

Shed

Some people have a shed "out back." Nowadays you can buy a portable shed, which is what one woman I know did. When we tackled her living room, stacked knee-high with piles of newspapers dating back to 1966, she simply bundled them up, gave me a sweet smile, and hauled them out to the shed where she restacked them. Her clutter problem wasn't solved, but when we were done you could reach the sofa and actually sit on it, which had been impossible before. Still another woman I know lived on a farm where she had a rather substantial chicken coop. She didn't have any chickens, so she scrubbed the coop down and loaded her boxed clutter into the coop. These women opted for what some people call design alternatives, and it's tough to argue with that.

Spare Room

The spare room ceases being spare when it is discovered by the pack rat. Everything and anything gets tossed into this room and when the room becomes impassable, the perpetrator simply closes the door and pretends it doesn't even exist. This can be maddening to the average decorator who is dying to get in there and redo the room.

Under the House

I had never really considered under the house storage until I came face to face with it through one of my clients. I organized a major move for one client that involved several days of packing before the actual move. On the day of the move, she very sweetly asked the movers to get a few things she had stored under the house. Two guys trundled down to the spot and spent forty-five minutes bringing out what seemed to be an unending pile of *stuff,* which we had to either repack or throw away since so much of it was ruined or badly damaged. Of course, since no decorator would be caught dead under a house, fear of getting caught is reduced substantially. Clutter can be stored there like dead bodies, rotting until the day of reckoning—that is, moving day. It's a horrible way for clutter to die, and it gives me the creeps.

Whatever your design scheme, it's never too late (as any decorator will happily tell you) to start over. By taking design principles from the get-organized-clean-sweep school, you can be your own decorator. Under all that clutter probably lies a space dying to be used, noticed, and enjoyed.

The Cost of Clutter

The cost of clutter can be a real killer. Clutter that never gets used gets stored. And storage space costs money whether it's in your closets, garage, basement, or a storage unit. After all, what do you think your monthly rent or mortgage payment pays for? *Space,* that's what it pays for! Think about it. How much space is required to hold those magazines and newspapers going back two years? Three square feet? Four square feet? And that's just the newspapers and magazines. How about the clothes you never wear? Are they using up two feet or five feet of hanging closet space? What about all those papers going back twenty years? They may be in boxes in the garage, but those boxes are still costing you money for the square footage they occupy. Is your never-used clutter taking up 10 percent of your space? 20 percent? 30 percent? Some simple arithmetic will show you how much of your monthly payment goes to store useless clutter. Just figure the percentage. If your monthly payment is $650 and your clutter controls 10 percent of your space, you are paying $65 per month for clutter, or $780 per year.

If you've reached the point where you think you have to move because you "need more space," think again. How much more money per month is that extra space going to cost you? $100? $200? $500? Unless you have three extra children with no place to sleep, it's a good bet that all you need the extra space for is to store your expanding cache of clutter.

It doesn't take an accountant to figure out that you can save money by eliminating clutter. First, you won't have to move, which will save you moving costs, deposit expenses, and/or escrow costs. Then you'll save the money you would have added to your monthly rental or housing payment. (Don't forget to multiply that times twelve to come up with your yearly savings.) Now, add the yearly savings to the moving, deposit and/or escrow savings for a total (savings) amount. With that eye-opening figure fixed firmly in your mind, take an honest inventory of your clutter.

Finally, do the only sensible and financially prudent thing: Chuck, give, or otherwise get rid of all the useless clutter that is currently occupying that expensive square footage. Take the money you will save yourself over the next clutter-free, don't-have-to-move year and invest it. Then watch your money — instead of your clutter — grow.

CLUTTER QUIZ

If you are still a little uncertain about your clutter quotient, grab a pen or pencil (if you can find one) and take this quiz. It's divided into categories so you can see clearly which clutter department presents the biggest challenge for you.

CLOTHES HORSE

1. Do you often have a problem figuring out what to wear even though your closet is full of clothes? **YES** ✓ **NO** ___

2. Do you hang on to clothes that haven't fit in years or are hopelessly out of date? **YES** ✓ **NO** ___

3. Do you have an Imelda Marcos situation breeding on your closet floor (i.e., piles of shoes dating back to the platform era)? **YES** ___ **NO** ✓

4. Do you own shoes that hurt your feet? **YES** ___ **NO** ✓

5. Do you have a collection of hats you rarely, if ever, wear? **YES** ___ **NO** ✓

6. Do you own more than two pairs of eyeglasses dating back several prescriptions? **YES** ✓ **NO** ___

7. Does your handbag or briefcase weigh more than five pounds? **YES** ___ **NO** ✓

8. Do you own enough earrings, necklaces, bracelets, rings, brooches, cufflinks, and stick pins to rival a pirate's treasure, the bulk of which you never wear? **YES** ✓ **NO** ___

9. Do you save makeup that has dried up, caked over, or dissolved almost to dust? **YES** ✓ **NO** ___

10. Do you own enough cosmetics to supply the cast of the floor show at Caeser's Palace for a month? **YES** ✓ **NO** ___

PAPER-NOIA

11. Do you keep piles of newspapers and magazines you haven't read because there's something that you must read in each paper or magazine? **YES** ✓ **NO** ___

12. Do you have more than one hundred copies of *National Geographic?* YES ___ NO ✓

13. Do you keep junk mail for weeks or even months at a time? YES ✓ NO ___

14. Do you have mail-order catalogs dating back several seasons? YES ___ NO ✓

15. Do you have so many books that you've started storing them in boxes? YES ___ NO ✓

16. Does the top of your desk look like the national archives? Is it so cluttered with piles of paper that you don't have any space left to do your work? YES ___ NO ✓

17. Have you ever filed something on Monday and been unable to find it again on Wednesday? YES ✓ NO ___

18. Do you have more than one calendar for the current year? Do you save calendars from years gone by? YES ✓ NO ___

19. Has your telephone, electricity, or other utility been turned off, or have your credit cards been stopped, simply because you lost the bill, and not because you didn't have the money? YES ___ NO ✓

20. Do you have a bulletin board with more than one layer of papers on it? Are you always running short on push pins? YES ___ NO ✓

21. Do you sometimes miss phone messages because whoever took the call couldn't find a pencil to write it down with? YES ___ NO ✓

22. Have you ever missed an important meeting or social event because you misplaced the invitation? YES ___ NO ✓

23. Is the information in your address book or Rolodex current? (Are there any names that you haven't the foggiest notion who those people are?) YES ✓ NO ___

CHEF-O-MATIC

24. Do you own appliances, gadgets, or gizmos that you never use? YES ✓ NO ___

25. Do you have uncounted brown paper bags lurking in a closet somewhere or squished into the corner between the wall and the refrigerator?   **YES** ___ **NO** ✓

26. Did the pots and pans stage an outright revolt the last time you opened the kitchen cupboard?   **YES** ___ **NO** ✓

27. Do you have enough plastic containers to store an entire month of leftovers, and then some?   **YES** ___ **NO** ✓

28. Do you own more than two sets of dishes? **YES** ✓ **NO** ___

29. Do you have more than one can opener or spatula? Do you have other duplicate kitchen utensils?   **YES** ✓ **NO** ___

KID STUFF

30. Do your kids own enough toys, games, and stuffed animals to outfit a toy store?   **YES** ___ **NO** ___

31. Are you still saving baby clothes and toys that your children outgrew years ago?   **YES** ___ **NO** ___

32. Do you have two tons of papers that your child dragged home from kindergarten through high school?   **YES** ___ **NO** ___

JUST WANT TO HAVE FUN

33. Do you have craft supplies and half-finished projects stashed all over the house?   **YES** ✓ **NO** ___

34. Are you a budding artist who gives art supplies squatter's rights in every room?   **YES** ___ **NO** ✓

35. Do you have material and patterns you haven't used in years?
                                                        YES ✓ **NO** ___

36. Do you have hundreds of photos that still haven't been put in albums?   **YES** ✓ **NO** ___

37. Is sports equipment stashed all over your house, from the hall closet to the basement to your bedroom?   **YES** ___ **NO** ✓

COLLECTOR

38. Do you have a collection of figurines, matchbooks, stuffed animals, rocks, hats, bottle caps, salt and pepper shakers, or Star Trek memorabilia? (HINT: It doesn't matter what you collect, we're interested in the acquisitive urge here.)   YES___ NO _✓_

39. Do you have boxes of heirlooms — china, table linens, quilts, furniture, knickknacks — stored somewhere on the premises?
YES _✓_ NO___

DO-IT-YOURSELFER

40. Can you lay your hands on a screwdriver or hammer within sixty seconds?   YES _✓_ NO___

41. How about hardware — can you find the right sizes of nails and screws as well?   YES _✓_ NO___

42. Do you tell everyone not to touch a thing in your shop because, in spite of the apparent mess, you know exactly where everything is?   YES _✓_ NO___

43. Do you save odd scraps of lumber because they're perfectly good, even though you have no immediate use for them?
YES _✓_ NO___

44. Do you know where your extension cords are right now?
YES _✓_ NO___

45. Do you ever save almost-dead batteries "for an emergency"?
YES___ NO _✓_

HOME SWEET CLUTTER

46. Do you have enough candles to outfit the whole neighborhood in case of a power outage?   YES___ NO _✓_

47. Are your linens stacked in precarious piles that inevitably topple over, so the neatly folded towels and sheets and placemats and pillowcases all end up in a jumbled mess?   YES___ NO _✓_

48. Do you have old prescriptions or outdated over-the-counter remedies in your medicine chest?   YES _✓_ NO___

49. Have you ever had to rewash clean clothes because they hadn't been put away and someone threw dirty clothes in with them? YES ✓ NO ___

50. Are you saving the box the stereo or microwave came in, along with enough gift boxes to provide for an entire hospital ward next Christmas? YES ✓ NO ___

51. Are your holiday decorations presentable when you get them out? Or are they broken, smashed, crumpled, or otherwise woebegone, so every year you end up replacing them? YES ✓ NO ___

52. Does your hall closet burst at the seams with clutter like Fibber McGee's? YES ___ NO ✓

53. Is the furniture slowly staging a hostile takeover of your house? Do you feel like you can't turn around without bumping into something? YES ___ NO ✓

54. Do you have things that have needed to be repaired, mended, or cleaned for months? YES ✓ NO ___

55. Do you have more than one "junk drawer"? YES ✓ NO ___

56. Is there more than one clock in any given room of your house (all showing different times)? YES ✓ NO ___

57. Is your attic or basement full of spare bed parts, broken lamps, old yearbooks, suitcases, uniforms, trophies, heirlooms— and what else you aren't sure? YES ✓ NO ___

58. Do you have maps for all fifty states in the glove box of your car? YES ___ NO ✓

59. Is the trunk of your car so full of junk that there's no room for the spare tire? YES ___ NO ✓

60. Is your garage so full of stuff there's no room for the car? YES ___ NO ✓

61. Do you have piles of things in your home or office? Are things stuffed under the bed, stacked in boxes, or packed in bags, all waiting until you have time to sort everything and decide where to put it? (You keep telling yourself if only . . . if only I had the time . . . if only I had more closet space . . . if only I had a bigger office. Do you have the "if only's"?) YES ✓ NO ___

62. Do you routinely lose or misplace things amongst your clutter? YES ✓ NO ___

63. Have you ever bought a new version of something you already own, simply because you couldn't find it? YES ✓ NO ___

64. Do you hold on to things just because someone gave them to you as a gift, and not because you actually like them? YES ✓ NO ___

65. Do you have so many possessions that you must rent additional storage space to store them all? YES ___ NO ✓

66. Is the clutter in your life so overwhelming that you don't know where to begin? YES ✓ NO ___

SCORING:

In an effort to keep things simple, give yourself one point for each YES.

IF YOUR SCORE IS:

1-10 Good. You're probably not overwhelmed with clutter, but chances are you've got a few hot spots. Just turn to the category of clutter in this book that describes your problem, and nip the clutter in the bud.

11-30 Uh Oh. Clutter is probably starting to put a permanent crease in your brow. You'll need to study more than a few sections of this book and make a real commitment to change.

31-50 Red Alert. You've got a clutter crisis on your hands. Chaos is probably a way of life for you. Read this entire book and train yourself to live by the guidelines for conquering and controlling clutter, or clutter will certainly continue to control you.

It Could Always Be Worse

Okay, maybe you've come to the conclusion that you are an out-of-control clutterbug. Maybe you're even feeling bad about how bad your clutter is. But don't feel bad on my account. However high your clutter is stacked, I'll bet I've seen worse. As a professional organizer, I've seen it all. Eventually clutter reaches the point where it sends the owner (and perpetrator) into an immobilizing coma. That's when they call me, the ultimate Clutterbuster. I've seen some mountains of clutter that looked insurmountable. But even the worst cases can be fixed. Let me tell you about some of my more memorable clients.

Francis and Her Fright Room

Francis is one of my favorite clients. Married to a famous musician, she does her best to be the perfect wife and mother, but clutter keeps getting the better of her. Papers, toys, photographs (she's a photo nut), records, tapes, CDs, and assorted memorabilia start to pile up the second she turns away from it. In desperation, she throws the stuff into an unused bedroom that has been dubbed the "Fright Room." When a family member starts looking for something among the clutter, they pray that it didn't get delegated to the fright room, because once something disappears in there, it might as well be gone forever. Fright room clutter is allowed to accumulate until it is chin-high and getting into the room is unthinkable. Then Francis calls me. I do battle with Francis's fright room fairly regularly, and her family is always happy to see me coming up the walk.

A Moving Experience

One of my nicest clients was Artie, who had a moving experience with me. His house was being renovated, and his architect kept insisting that he move his furniture, art collection, and other belongings out of the house. Artie stalled until he could stall no longer. Finally, he called me and I moved Artie's stuff out of the house and into storage. I had to hire a special crew to pack and move the art. Another crew packed everything else. Moving men moved everything except the art (which got moved first). During that week, Artie would periodically pop in long enough to wail, "How did I accumulate all of this stuff?" He'd write out checks and beat a hasty retreat, leaving me to continue packing, logging, and storing his things. Artie was the most cooperative client I've ever worked with—he couldn't get away from the scene of the clutter fast enough. And he had a sense of humor, which was good, because all told, the move to storage cost him over $5,000, and subsequent storage costs are running in the neighborhood of $500 per month. That's not all. The architect keeps changing the date when Artie can move back in, so it looks like it will be at least eight months instead of five months before Artie can ransom his things out of storage and spend another $5,000 or so to move back in. He'll call me to do it, I know, and then he and I will get to have another moving experience together.

Susan and Her Storage Units

Susan is an upstanding member of Beverly Hills whose name (along with her husband's) is often in the society columns. Money is no object for Susan, so she buys whatever she wants whenever she wants. This buying frenzy manifests itself daily, either by going to shops, ordering from catalogs, or having merchandise delivered for her perusal. But once she's purchased these things, she doesn't know where to put it all. Never one to let something like clutter stand in her way, Susan simply shifted to storage. As new merchandise came in, she had other household items put in a self-storage unit. Eventually, she had seven units (in addition to her very large Beverly Hills casa), and duplications all over the place. She would buy a new comforter, even though there were already three in storage. Or, if she was a little disappointed in the color of something she ordered from a catalog, she'd send it to storage for use "later." Susan called me to inventory everything in storage units and keep track of it—an ongoing process since Susan was forever sending or retrieving something to or from storage. The most incredible thing about Susan and her storage units was that she managed to juggle all of this clutter on an almost daily basis, at the cost of thousands of dollars per month, without her husband ever knowing about it. After a couple of years, her husband did start to wonder about where the money was, and Susan decided to bite the bullet and have a giant garage sale. She located an empty two-story house to display her clutter so she could sell it. There was so much, the house was full. She hired people to come in and run the sale. I figure the cost of her clutter, plus the storage units, plus me to keep it all organized, plus the people to run the sale, minus the money she took in on the sale, probably left her about twenty thousand dollars *in the hole.* I haven't heard from her since the sale, but I've got a feeling the clutter habit will kick back in any day now, and she'll start ordering storage units again. That's the day Susan will pick up the phone and dial my number. It will be just like old times.

Hilda and the Health Department

When Hilda called me, she said it was because she had heard me speak at a function she'd attended. But when I saw Hilda's house, I knew the real reason. Although she denied it, I knew somebody had called the health department. Clutter in boxes, bags, piles, and stacks covered Hilda's two bedroom house from one end to the other. A path had been maintained to get from room to room, and that was it. Rat droppings covered the kitchen counters, the floors around the baseboards, and even her bed. There were holes in the wall, and mildew permeated the air. The windows had to be forced open so we could get some air. The family room, which lead to the breezeway, was impassable. Her daughter came by after we cleared that room and was so delighted that she could see the piano (for the first time in years) that she immediately sat down and played for us. The breezeway had clutter, including things like a kitchen sink, piled to the ceiling. It was a terrifying sight indeed. And the garage was not much better. We did what we could for Hilda. Over the many days that we were there, she kept insisting that someone else, not she, had made this mess. In the end, even this professional organizer had her limit. We didn't go near the breezeway.

Pat the Pack Rat

Pat, like so many other clutterbugs, saved everything. She had cartons and piles of things all over the house. Her bathroom was jam-packed with bottles and jars of potions — ten bottles of the same shampoo and fourteen tubes of toothpaste — and her kitchen was no better. Dozens and dozens of exotic spices and bottles of cleaning fluids I had never heard of were in every cabinet. Her clothes went back decades and four sizes. She saved herbs and twigs, old catalogs, papers, cards, you name it. Even though this woman refused to get rid of anything, we went in and organized her. At the end of the day, she'd put on gloves and go through the garbage to reassure herself that I had not thrown away something important. She even kept her cat's whiskers as they fell (naturally) off his fuzzy little face. I bagged, tagged, boxed, filed, and in general, organized everything for this woman. It took us ten days to do her house. When we were finished, the difference was so astonishing that she had a party for her friends to show off her newly organized habitat.

Julie's Twelve-Year Time Capsule

Julie is a wife and mother of the first order. She lives with her doctor husband, two perfectly behaved children, and an adorable pet dog in a large house situated on a beautifully wooded lot in Connecticut. This picturesque setting began to tilt when Julie became so busy that she more or less stopped getting rid of as much as she might have and gradually gave up the concept of household organization altogether. Time passed, and Julie's clutter grew. Several key areas in the house were clutter-choked, particularly the pantry (no one had seen the floor of the pantry in years), the kitchen counters, the bathroom, the closets, and every available surface in the master bedroom. Julie's family loved her—of that there was no doubt—but making their way through the clutter on a daily basis was becoming too much. When her husband decided to add a new wing onto the house, he put his foot down. Julie's clutter problem would *not*, under any circumstances, be permitted to move into the new space. Since part of the new space included a master bedroom, it was clear that Julie would need help figuring out what could be moved into the new bedroom from the old bedroom and how to organize everything else that had been clogged with clutter. She told herself she was ready to get organized for the new wing. But she also told herself she was ready because it was the best thing to do for her family. The clutter was driving them crazy, and even though the clutter really didn't bother her, she decided to do whatever was necessary to give her loved ones some relief.

Julie, like so many other people who call me, had a bit of a problem accurately describing the scope of her clutter. Based on her verbal description and a few snapshots she sent me, I thought that perhaps five days would get her house in order. I was more than a little surprised to discover that over the years, Julie had stored up what amounted to a virtual clutter time-capsule. Things seemed to go back ten to twelve years everywhere we looked and in every room of the house. There was a closet full of eight-year-old maternity clothes; there was a pair of two-toned purple suede platform shoes that were at least twelve years old if they were a day. There were monster piles of clutter in the bathroom ("hidden" under sheets and towels) that featured makeup of every description in various stages of years-old decay. The children's toys had been kept in perpetuity since babyhood in the downstairs rec room (the kids were now nine and eleven years old). And everywhere were papers, papers, papers. Receipts, scraps with phone numbers on them, old school schedules, newspaper clippings, stacks and stacks of catalogues, hundreds of clipped recipes all co-mingled everywhere (in every room) with coupons and money-saving box tops that had been clipped and cut years ago and never redeemed.

Julie and I dived into the clutter. I was determined, and she was committed. By the time the week was over, we had filled thirty-two of the largest trash bags available and put together a good three carloads of stuff to go to charity. In only one week, Julie and I ruthlessly weeded out and organized her clutter. Julie heroically let go of an enormous amount of ancient clutter, and she did it virtually cold turkey. But it was tough. The hardest day for me was when we started finding, among other things, the hundreds of pieces of paper in the pantry and then the bathroom (those are not your normal places for stashing paper, after all). It was then that I knew that there was no way we would be able to go through and organize all twelve years' worth of paper along with all of the other clutter that needed to be dealt with. (In the end, we boxed what paper we couldn't go through, and I went back later to help her tackle those leftover papers). Every single day was tough for Julie. She worked non-stop for six to eight hours each day. We barely stopped to eat. She threw or gave away things that I know made her heart and stomach ache. The day I suggested she let her children decide which, if any, baby toys they wanted to hang onto was probably her worst day. With trembling hands, she allowed the children to make their choices. They gave almost all of the outdated toys away, and I saved a small selection of the toys for mom. I know she died a little bit that day, but she did it for her family. They just couldn't take the clutter any more. Her husband called me the Mother Theresa of organizing, but in my book, she was the most courageous client I've ever met.

And there've been others. I've worked with small businesses that were started by some geniuses who thought all they needed to be successful were great ideas and relatives to answer the telephones. I've organized the paperwork for divorce cases, for property transactions, investments, and lawsuits. I've straightened out the bills as well as the personal paperwork for clients. I've tackled clutter in closets and garages, and I've worked for all types of people. I've heard and seen it all.

My experiences have taught me that certain principles apply to all clutter and that one pack rat is pretty much like another pack rat, give or take a few idiosyncrasies. I know, for example, that it is unrealistic to expect clutterbugs to get rid of *all* of their clutter. People aren't willing to take everything and chuck it into the trash just because someone else tells them to. So I don't tell people to throw away their clutter . . . oh, I may strongly *suggest* it, but the decision is up to the clutter's owner, not to me.

If you are ready to start making some decisions and taking action with your own clutter, a good starting point is the *Ten Commandments on Clutter:*

Ten Commandments on Clutter

I. STOP PROCRASTINATING

Stop putting off until tomorrow what you can do today, especially since you know you probably won't do it tomorrow anyway. *Decide to decide* what you are going to do with the next piece of clutter that you pick up. And stop stashing clutter all over the place *for now.*

II. QUIT MAKING EXCUSES

Stop making tiresome excuses for your clutter. You are only fooling yourself.

III. USE IT OR LOSE IT

If you're not using it, get rid of it. Period.

IV. LEARN TO LET GO

As lives change, needs change, but somehow clutter accumulates with no regard for our changed perspective. Clutter that is merely taking up valuable space and giving you nothing in return should be tossed or given away.

V. BE A GIVER

Give things away, right away. Don't wait until you die to give away china that you don't use now while you're alive. Every garment in your closet that you never wear could be worn by a less fortunate person. Friends, relatives, and charities all appreciate a giving person far more than they do a pack rat.

VI. SET LIMITS

Limit the amount of space you allocate to house your clutter. Closets, bookcases, filing cabinets — all should be limited. Just because one space fills up doesn't mean you should find or buy more space for more clutter. It means that it's time to weed out your current accumulation so you can reclaim the space you already have.

VII. USE THE IN & OUT INVENTORY RULE

If something new comes in, something old goes out. Apply this rule to everything from toys and clothes to books and magazines. Stick to it, and you'll always be in control of your clutter.

VIII. LESS IS MORE

The less clutter you have, the more time, money, and energy you will have. People will stop nagging you, and you'll be under less stress and be more productive in the end.

IX. KEEP EVERYTHING IN ITS PLACE

Find a place for everything and keep everything in its place. (The blender does not belong in the bedroom and the mail does not belong in the bathroom.)

X. COMPROMISE

Compromise when you are organizing your clutter. Stop letting your perfectionism keep you from doing or letting someone else help you dispense with your clutter. Functioning efficiently is more important than functioning perfectly. Remember that perfect is not the same as excellent, and sometimes good is good enough.

I know you can conquer and control your clutter. You can get rid of what you don't need, and organize what you can't bear to part with so that you can spend your time living life instead of caring for your clutter. All in all, it's a good life when you come out from under the clutter!

Surviving a Mine Field of Clutter Traps

Even the best intentioned can be waylaid by a clutter trap that litters your path in life. Stepping gingerly around these traps can save you from clutter and all its consequences. Some of the most dangerous clutter traps are:

> FLEA MARKETS
>
> GARAGE SALES
>
> GIFT SHOPS
>
> RUMMAGE SALES
>
> SALES OF ANY KIND
>
> SOUVENIR SHOPS

If you find yourself being drawn inexplicably to any of these traps, call a friend or relative to talk you down. Otherwise you'll be "picking up a little something" that is known to saner souls as clutter. It will be useless or silly, and you won't have a place to put it. It won't go with anything, or you'll have to clean it or fix it first before it is perfect. You've been booby trapped, and you are the booby. So start getting control of your clutter habit now by avoiding what can only bring you clutter and the grief that goes along with it.

Developing Your Battle Plan

If you're ready to get organized and can't quite figure out where to begin, you'll need to start by setting up the proper attitude and atmosphere. While you're dealing with your clutter, put the following rules into effect:

- •**Don't allow distractions.** No visitors, TV, or stopping to read an article in a magazine you pick up.
- •**No phone calls.** Don't take any and don't make any.

•**Stay out of the kitchen.** Stop to eat only at meal time.

•**Do one thing at a time.** If you are cleaning out a closet, just work on that closet; don't walk into another room and start doing something else until you are finished with that closet.

•**Don't try to keep everything!** Hoarding is physically and mentally exhausting, and you'll never conquer your clutter unless you can learn to let go.

•**If you're having trouble finding the time to get things done,** try reading my first book, *How to Get Organized When You Don't Have the Time.*

A Place for Everything

One of the keys to clutter control is to have a place for everything. This can be difficult when clutter has usurped nearly every available space, creating an unending mass of confusion. Caught hopelessly in the middle of the muddle, the bewildered owner/perpetrator can barely begin to figure out where to start, much less find a place for everything. These guidelines should help you get along, then figure out what belongs where.

1. **First, commit to organizing the clutter in one complete area without stopping** (such as a room or a closet), knowing that you may have to spend a significant amount of time on your project. Either set aside a half day (minimum) or tell yourself that you won't stop until two closets or the garage or the bathrooms are done.

2. **Set up large cardboard cartons labeled CHARITY, TOSS, and ELSEWHERE.** That way, when you come across something that goes in another room, you can put it in the ELSEWHERE box, and put those things in the proper room at the end of the day. Otherwise you'll end up running all over the house, interrupting yourself over and over as you transfer items to other rooms.

3. **Next, empty the target area of all clutter.** Pull it out into another area (the hall or onto the bed) sorting as you go.

4. **If you're not sure where something belongs,** think about keeping items as close to their point of first use as possible.

Dishes should be in cabinets near the sink or dishwasher, pens and paper belong near the telephones and in the desk, and videotapes should be kept near the VCR. (Also keep duplicate items where it would make sense. Keeping scissors in the bathroom and on the desk can eliminate searching for and moving the scissors every time you need to clip something.)

5. **What's left stays in that room's closet.** Remember to group like items together and keep them in clutter containers (i.e., all of the underwear goes in the same area with drawer dividers to keep it separated, and all of the bobby pins and hair clips go together in containers in one area).

6. **When you are finished, take the contents of the TOSS box out to the trash.** Bag it tightly so that no one in the family can dig through it to retrieve items. Put the CHARITY box in the car, and the next time you go out, drop it off. Put the box marked ELSEWHERE into the hall to be sorted and carried to other rooms.

7. **Reward yourself when you are done,** and keep repeating this process until you have licked all of the clutter in your life. The reward system is limited only by your desires and imagination. Some possible rewards that you can give yourself are:
      Lunch at an expensive restaurant
      A massage
      A gigantic ice cream sundae
      An afternoon movie
      A round of golf
      A facial
      A manicure and/or pedicure
      A day at the beach or park with a good book
      An evening out at a concert or a play

8. **In the future, when clutter starts to get out of control,** stop and take twenty minutes to pick up the room. Put everything in the right room—you can put it away within that room later. Toys go in the kids' room or the playroom, dirty clothes and towels go in the hamper or laundry room, dirty

dishes go in the dishwasher, papers and magazines go in a reading stack, and jackets go in the coat closet. Later, when you have more time, you can put things away more specifically (toys in toy chest, unread newspapers in trash, etc.).

9. **Always be looking for ways to make effective and creative use of clutter storage containers,** boxes, racks, and bins. Trunks and functional furniture that can hold items and also be used as furniture can help you designate specific places for clutter. For instance, games can be stored in a trunk that can also be used as a game table for children by placing a table top on the trunk.

10. **Make an ongoing effort to get rid of things you never use,** so that those things don't pile up into clutter mounds that you keep moving from place to place. A CHARITY box should always be on hand to hold those items. The minute it gets full, bag the items and get them out of the house and down to the charity's location. Let them deal with the clutter you don't need.

Follow these guidelines and, believe it or not, you too will find yourself with a place for everything, and everything in its place.

How to Use This Book

If you survived the quiz, it's a good bet that you're ready to commit yourself to your own clutter countdown. Rather than flipping a coin to determine where to start, you'll want to glance back at the results of the quiz.

Then flip to the category of clutter that is giving you the most trouble. All of the categories are listed alphabetically, so if you've got mountains of magazines, for example, turn to the M's. Most clutter categories are noted with a *see also.* These cross-references will direct you to another category of clutter that you might be having trouble with. For example, under *Magazines,* you'll find *see also Desk, Mail, and National Geographic.* Many people who have trouble with magazine clutter also have trouble with desk clutter and mail clutter, and, for *National Geographic* subscribers, there's a category of clutter for that magazine all its own. So check the *see also*'s to see if another clutter hot spot of yours is noted.

If it is, you can turn to that section for more information on how to tackle that area of clutter as well. Since clutter tends to spread from one area and category to another, the chances are good that you'll be flipping to more than a few *see also* cross-references. Some of the principles are repeated throughout the book; this is because overlapping areas of clutter often benefit from the same clutter control techniques (i.e., *Mail* and *Papers*).

As you work on weeding out and eliminating your clutter, refer to the Storage: Clutter Containers sections, where you'll find descriptions of lots of inexpensive storage ideas to help you contain your must-keep clutter. For help in how to give away or recycle your clutter, see Recycling Your Clutter Cast-offs in the back of the book. And the Resource Helpline section gives you the names and addresses of organizing professionals and manufacturers or organizational products and systems. You'll be able to turn to these resources as you start reorganizing and storing the clutter that you can't bear to part with.

Finally, after you've used this reference guide to conquer your clutter problem areas, you can use the Clutterbusters to Live By to keep the remaining clutter, along with any incoming clutter, under control.

It couldn't be simpler, really. Just read what you need when you need it. An application of the principles and tips in this book, along with some determination and consistent effort on your part, could mean a new you. Once you've become organized and have a clutter-free environment, you'll have lots of time to put your best foot forward without tripping over the clutter. So what are you waiting for? On your mark, get set, go!

Clutter from A to Z

> **MESS** A state of disarray, especially a condition of untidy confusion; an embarrassing situation or muddle; a dirty or disagreeable concoction; a hodgepodge; a confused, unkempt, or offensive condition. Or, according to your mother-in-law, the sum total of who and what you are, as in, "Good Lord, you're a mess . . . just look at this house!"

Addresses
(see Business Cards, Phone Numbers)

Announcements
(see also Bulletin Boards, Calendars,
Desk, Mail, Papers)

Announcements and invitations all too often get lost in the general incoming mail clutter. Before you know it, you've missed that art opening or wedding shower you wanted to attend. Weeks after the event, you come across the announcement or invitation and stare stupidly at it, annoyance mounting steadily. To avoid repeating this performance, open your mail when it comes and make a decision about the event on the spot. Check your calendar, and if you have the time available and want to attend the event, mark it on the calendar. Put the announcement (or invitation) either in the back of your calendar if you have a desk calendar (highly recommended), or in a basket near the calendar if you have a wall calendar.

If you use only a briefcase, purse, or pocket-type calendar, keep the invitations in a colored folder in an easily accessible place, such as on top of your desk in a rack, or in the very front of your desk file drawer.

When the date rolls around, simply pull out the announcements so that you have all of the pertinent details and directions at hand. Now take a shower, comb your hair, and *go*.

Antiques
(see also Collections, Heirlooms)

I used to be in the antique business, so you won't get an argument
from me about the value of some of your great grandmother's
heirlooms. People get into trouble, however, when they start packing
and storing antiques, thinking that they are going to either sell them
someday or pass them along as heirlooms to their relatives.
Generally these items get stored in the attic, basement, or garage,
and eventually bugs, mildew, damp conditions, and mice wreak
havoc, turning beautiful things into useless junk. The solution is to
use and display your antiques. If you don't want or have room to do
this, then sell them *now*. And if your antiques are packed just so
you can pass them on to your heirs, why not pass them along right
now so they can be put to use and be appreciated on a daily basis?

Appliances
(see also Gadgets, Kitchen Utensils, Pots & Pans)

In our quest for labor- and time-saving devices, we often grab for
the newest fandangled gadget on the market, adding to our
inventory of appliances. Can openers, crock pots, blenders,
coffeemakers, toasters, juicers, warmers, grinders, deep fryers, food
processors, carving knives, popcorn poppers, salad shooters, egg
poachers, pasta makers, french fry cutters, and of course, the mighty
microwave, are just a few of the possible appliances found in the
average home. All of these appliances require electricity, and the
average kitchen has a decided shortage of outlets and counter space
to accommodate these gadgets. If you must have a plethora of
electrical appliances (c'mon now, how often do you really use that
egg poacher?), you might want to invest in a kitchen center that
provides additional storage as well as work space. (Some models
also feature extra electrical outlets.)

This portable cabinet is generally made of wood or metal, and
has storage space in the form of shelves and extra countertop work
space. Many of these cabinets roll on casters, and some feature
butcher block tops to provide an area for cutting and preparing
food. Appliances can be stored in the cabinet, pulled out and
plugged into the extra outlet provided, and put to use on the extra
countertop space. Some appliances, such as coffeemakers, toasters,
and can openers, can now be mounted under wall cabinets, which
means that your countertops remain clear for other food
preparation activities.

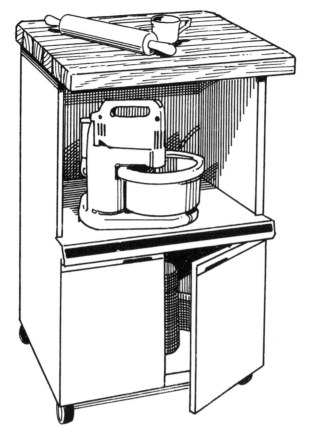

© Closet Maid Serving Cart by Clairson International, 720 S.W. 17th St., Ocala FL 32674

But the best organizational idea of all for appliances is to get rid of some of them. If it's shoved into the back of the cabinet, if it's too complicated to use, or if you never use it because, on the rare occasions that you need it, it's just too much trouble to dig it out and put it away again, get rid of it. Now is the time to deal with the broken appliances as well. If you're like most people, you hang onto them, thinking that as soon as you get around to it, you'll get it repaired. In theory, this makes perfect sense. In reality, the broken appliance gets stuffed into the far reaches of some cabinet, never to be seen again. Even after it gets replaced, the broken appliance, for some incomprehensible reason, stays put. You *need* that cabinet space, so either throw the broken item out or give it to a charity that repairs the items they take in. If your appliances have turned to clutter rather than contributing daily to your food preparation, now is the time to go back to simpler times in your kitchen by dumping the appliances that have become albatrosses.

Art & Art Supplies
(see also Craft Supplies, Paint & Paintbrushes)

If you or a member of your family is a budding artist, the question of what to do with art supplies can be a vexing one. Art supply stores sell elaborate boxes, cabinets, and taborets to hold paints, brushes, and artwork, but they can be expensive. A little imagination can go a long way here. Adapt a ceramic vase, coffee can, or large oatmeal box to hold brushes, or use an inexpensive tackle or tool box to control some of your colorful artistic clutter. These supply containers can be stored on a shelf built near your work area or in a closet (where the items are stored). A narrow shelf will do the trick and take up a minimum amount of space.

Rolling basket systems can become portable art centers for holding jars of paint, brushes, and art paper supplies. If you have art that can be rolled up, it can be stored in large, clean, circular trash cans, or in architect's bins (these bins are expensive, but look terrific). To store flat canvases, you might want to build a simple cabinet, or adapt one you already have by adding plywood partitions to make slots to slide the canvases into for storage. Or, you can turn a small bookcase on end to change it from a horizontal storage unit for books to a vertical storage unit for art. Finally, you don't have to keep every jar of dried up old paint just because you are a creative genius, nor do you need to keep every original work of art you've ever created. If it's so great, sell it, hang it on your own walls, or (be careful here) give it to a friend or relative.

ZIL•LION The number of excuses you'll come up with to *not* get rid of a specific item of clutter.

Baby Clothes
(see also Children, Closets, Stuffed Animals)

Whenever I think of baby clothes, I think of my client, Sue Ann. Sue Ann had two kids, a dog that wasn't housebroken, a bird, a husband, and clutter up to her eyebrows. A large part of the clutter stemmed from the baby clothes of the two kids. Sue Ann steadfastly refused to give those clothes up, citing her ongoing energetic efforts to conceive another child to add to the already chaotic clan. The fly in the ointment was her husband, who would yell from behind the kitchen door, "Sue Ann, get rid of these baby clothes—we are NOT having another baby!" In spite of her husband's obvious resistance, Sue Ann stubbornly refused to give up the baby clothes, and continues, as far as I know, to try to add to the family, firm in her conviction that those baby clothes will come in handy someday soon.

I've worked with more women than I care to count who refuse to part with their children's baby clothes, even though they know (unlike Sue Ann) that they are *not* having any more children. Their kids grow up, get married, go to college, and Mom still has cartons of baby clothes stacked in the back closet, attic, or garage. Only a mother could understand the significance of those clothes, which transcends anything that can be verbalized. Still, I'd like to suggest that to pack and store more than one small carton of any category of items for sentimental reasons is asking for trouble. Baby clothes in boxes that never get seen, appreciated, or used make me pause. I always suggest, very softly, "Mother, wouldn't it be a wonderful thing to give most of these to a family that is in need so that their child can enjoy these things today?" Select a few items for mementos, pack them nicely, and give the rest away.

Bags
(see also Closets, Shopping Bags)

Some people automatically keep shopping bags, paper bags, and plastic bags. They don't think about it, they just keep them. Like squirrels, bag keepers stash the bags in any number of places—in the closets, in linen cabinets, under the sink, and next to the refrigerator. Some people even start hanging them on the door-knobs of all the doors in the house. The old "I might need it someday" excuse is often called into action here. And the fact is, you really might need one of these bags sometime, maybe even this week. But you are *not* going to need the twenty-five brown paper bags stuffed between the refrigerator and the wall (along with the dust balls and bugs), and I doubt that you'll need the twelve shopping bags squashed in the hall closet behind the vacuum cleaner. Bags collect dust and bugs, and unless you are a hermit who never eats or shops, you can easily replace bags you throw away simply by going to the supermarket. So keep ten or twelve bags on hand if you must, but throw the rest away. Now.

Balls

*(see also Children, Exercise Equipment,
Sports Equipment)*

Baseballs, beachballs, basketballs, volleyballs, and balls for the cat and dog all seem like fun things to have, but storing them can be tricky. What usually happens is that they roll around the house, yard, car, and garage always in the way, and then either magically disappear or deflate just when you're about to deliver on your longstanding promise to shoot a few baskets with the kids. A simple solution to the ball problem is to buy a large plastic trash can and put it in the backyard or garage. Henceforth, all balls go in the can when not in use. Keep an air pump nearby for the inevitable flat surprises. Assuming you can train everybody to put the balls into the can, you won't have to worry about lost balls, or worse, somebody stumbling over a loose ball and breaking his neck or suing your socks off. Play ball!

Baskets

(see also Collections)

Baskets are terrific for holding things, so much so that they're included in the Storage: Clutter Containers section at the back of the book. But if you are a basket junkie, you have probably lost sight of the organizational potential of baskets. Baskets hanging from every ceiling and stacked in every corner may have started out as a good decorative idea, but invariably they become dust and clutter collectors, and you become known as a basket case. Put your baskets to use to hold groups of items and, except for a few decorative baskets, get rid of the rest.

Let baskets do double duty; they can be attractive and functional at the same time. Square or oblong baskets are the best bet since they hold more in less space than do round baskets.

Consider these storage possibilities for your baskets:
•Cosmetics (like lipsticks or brushes)
•Coupons
•Dry cleaning (separate from laundry basket)
•Hair ornaments and pins
•Jewelry
•Laundry
•Magazines and newspapers
•Mail
•Pens and pencils

- Postcards and greeting cards
- Stuffed animals
- Toys
- Yarn and crochet supplies

Bathroom Clutter
(see also Cosmetics)

The bathroom is the nerve center of the average household. And yet, it is often woefully under-equipped to serve the needs of all the people who pass through its portals. If more than two or three people use the same bathroom every day as their launching pad, confusion often reigns as eager participants wait their turn.

☑ CLUTTER CHECKLIST

You can reorganize your bathroom paraphernalia with the help of a few simple gadgets and techniques:

❑ **Shampoo Storage** — Get a portable shelf that loops over the shower head to hold shampoo supplies. This makes the shampoo easy to find, even with your eyes closed.

❑ **Rubber Duckie** — Use a tray to hold your rubber duckie, soap, and other miscellaneous scrub-a-dub items you want kept near the tub.

❑ **Junk Drawer** — Put divider trays into your bathroom drawers so that you can reasonably divide all of the small items that might otherwise get tangled up into one gigantic mess in the drawer. This is great for bobby pins, manicure equipment, hair accessories, cosmetics, and the toothpaste and/or toothbrushes. Cleaning the drawer becomes a simple matter of lifting the trays out and giving them a quick sudsing from time to time.

❑ **Round Table** — Use Lazy Susan systems to store bottles and jars in the bathroom cabinets. With deep cabinets, it's almost impossible to reach behind one bottle to get another without experiencing a frustrating collapse of everything. These revolving systems put an end to that frustration.

❑ **Wet Head** — Get a Lucite or plastic hair dryer holder and install it on the bathroom wall or inside your cabinet door. You'll be able to neatly store the hair dryer when not in use, and you'll always be able to find it when you need it.

The average family finds it difficult, if not impossible, to store the basic necessities for all of the family members in one bathroom. Rush hour for a typical bathroom on a weekday morning finds everybody lined up with an assortment of critical bathroom gear tucked under their arms—everything from makeup to rubber duckies to hot curlers. Once in the bathroom, each person *means* to take their clutter back out with them, but somehow that never happens. Left behind are cosmetics, creams, shampoos and conditioners, hot curlers and curling irons, razors, brushes, hairpins, colognes and aftershave potions, and bath toys. Towels and washcloths proliferate, both clean and dirty, and eventually the bathroom becomes a maze for all who enter. Ultimately, making the room efficiently comfortable and finding more space for the grooming essentials can be the key to conquering the clutter and making the bathroom a better place to be.

Since the bathroom often serves as the jumping off spot in the daily effort to just get started, conquering the clutter there can mean a cleaner, faster, and much calmer approach to yet another day.

Batteries
(see also Junk Drawer)

I don't know why we can't buy one battery at a time, but we can't. So, if you're like me, you rip open the package, take out what you need, and drop the rest into the first handy drawer or container. Then, when you need those extra batteries, you can't find them, so you go out and buy another package and repeat the entire process again. Short of shooting the battery manufacturers, the best solution seems to be to set up a "battery center." Dump all of your batteries into a container and store them in the refrigerator. The next time you only need one battery, you'll know where to find the extras, and since they are stored in the refrigerator, you have a better chance of finding one that works.

Books
(see also Recipes)

Books can accumulate with frightening results. Bookcases are all too easily overrun, and stacks of books start forming in cabinets, corners, and closets. Book-aholics very often feel that their book clutter is righteous clutter, indeed, *superior* clutter. The books add more to their image than to their intellect, however, since it is a rare, rare thing to find someone with hundreds of books who has actually read even a fraction of the books they own.

I used to feel very smug about my books. I had hundreds of books, spilling over (neatly, of course) into bookshelves all over the house. After all, didn't it prove that I was intelligent and worldly? Weren't my many interests displayed perfectly to go with the decor? I lived with my books and this smug attitude until the day I priced a move from the east coast to the west coast. Reality hit me in the head with a *thunk* that I never forgot. It was going to cost a small fortune to move those books and, faced with economic choices, I did the only sensible thing. I left 80 percent of the books behind; the other 20 percent made the move by fourth class mail.

Today I have one large bookcase and one small bookcase. The small bookcase holds my first editions, and the big bookcase holds everything else. When the large bookcase gets full, I bite the bullet and give some away before I allow myself to buy any more. This way, I keep my book habit under control.

Finally, with books, the Wait & Save Rule is a good one. Wait until the book comes out in paperback—you'll save money and space. Chances are your reading pile is backed up from here to eternity anyway, so waiting a little longer won't hurt. (See Clutter Checklist on pages 38 and 39.)

Boxes
(see also Holiday Decorations, Packing Materials)

Lots of people keep boxes because they might move someday. Or, they keep boxes that computer and stereo equipment were packed in—they'll definitely need that when they move! If you are one of these people, I'd like you to measure the square footage that these boxes occupy. Then, I'd like you to figure out the cost per square foot per year to store these empty boxes (refer back to page 10 if you need help with this). I'll bet you a doughnut that if you ever do move, it'll be as cheap to buy new boxes from the movers. Shoot, you'll probably *save* money. So get rid of those empty taking-up-expensive-space boxes. Oh, keep a couple if it'll make you feel better, but dump the rest. You don't want to move anyway.

The few boxes you keep can be stored inside of each other, or flattened out and stacked. Boxes that can be broken down in this matter and then reassembled either by fitting the notches together, folding them together, or taping them together are the best to keep because they take up the least amount of storage space, yet provide the same function when it comes time to use them.

✔ CLUTTER CHECKLIST

As you go through your books to weed out the ones you can live without, consider these thoughts about the following categories of books:

❏ **Children's Books** — If your kids have read these books and they don't care what happens to them, why should you? Give them to a charity that helps families so some other kids can enjoy them.

❏ **Cookbooks** — If you regularly use more than five recipes in each of your cookbooks, raise your hand You get to keep those books. If not, copy the few recipes you do use and a few more you might try someday and give the books away. We all know you can cook.

❏ **How-To Books** — If you read the how-to book and feel you need to refer back to it for reminder information or for motivation, then by all means keep it on the shelf. If you read the book and it made no sense or seemed silly, get rid of it. If you just plain forgot why you bought it in the first place, why keep it?

❏ **Phone Books** — I'm a big believer in information by phone, so if you like to while away the day by letting your fingers do the walking, fine. Just do it in the most recent phone book for your region. Throw the rest of those door-stoppers away.

❏ **Reference Books** — If you ever refer to them, reference books are great, and should be kept. If, on the other hand, you're keeping a complete set of the *Encyclopedia Britannica* just because it looks good, give yourself a break. Get rid of it, and use the shelf space for something else that contributes to your life.

❏ **Textbooks** — Get rid of these. No ifs, ands, or buts. They're outdated, you don't use them, and you never will.

❏ **Unread Books** — Eventually, you'll need to face up to your inventory of unread books — those books that you bought or received as a gift — you intend to read "someday soon." A profes-

Brochures
(see also Desk, Files & Filing Cabinets, Mail, Papers)

Brochures can represent dreams or nightmares. Brochures for that cruise you can't afford, and brochures pleading for help for the

sional organizer I know faced up to her unread books when a friend of hers demanded to know if she had read all of these books on her shelves. "Well, er, no," mumbled my friend the organizer, who right then and there decided to do something about those unread books. She went through all of her books and marked the unread books with little red stick-on dots. What she did *not* do was read the unread books. Normally a logical person, it did not occur to her then that the red dot system was not getting the books read. The folly of it all presented itself to her one day when, in reading a newsletter, she saw a bit of news she had no knowledge about. Calling the editor (who, as it happens, was me) she demanded to know why she hadn't been told about this ongoing news before. I pointed out that it had been reported in the previous newsletter, and, upon digesting this news, she realized that she must have "red-dotted" the previous newsletter, and therefore missed the initial reporting of the news altogether. Last I heard, she still had a lot of red-dotted books, but at least now she is laughing about the dots. I think she should read the books before she buys any more, or give them away. That's what I think you should do too.

❑ **Yearbooks**—These are my favorites, particularly the ones from high school. Really, how often do you refer to that photo of yourself, resplendent in cat-eye glasses and beehive hair, smiling goofily next to the class clown? Or is it those words of wisdom penned inside the book that keeps you from parting with these annual records of your anxious adolescence, such as "To Pat— You're a real sweet girl"? On the one hand, I think these books serve a legitimate nostalgic purpose—if you were the class president or the head cheerleader. But if you are like most people, high school left a lot to be desired, so, all things considered, why keep memories in your den or living room of what was essentially a lackluster experience?

mountain goats in Timbuktu tend to make your paper clutter picturesque, if nothing else. If you really think you'll have the money for that cruise soon, keep the brochure in a box or file it along with other travel stuff (that you probably haven't looked at since you started clipping it). Brochures asking for your money or your vote should be read, paid (put them in your TO PAY basket — see *Mail* and *Papers* — so you can pay it when you next pay bills), and/or immediately discarded.

Bulletin Boards
(see also Announcements, Business Cards, Calendars, Cards, Notes, Phone Numbers, Postcards)

If you really want to clutter up your life, get a bulletin board. Then do what everyone else does with it; start sticking things up there that you either "need" or like to look at. Initially you tell yourself that you will stick (and *stick* is the key word here) critical I-need-to-be-reminded-of-this items on the board. This visual tickler system evaporates as soon as you start automatically impaling postcards from Florida, cartoons that are politically significant to your life and times, telephone numbers, and assorted schedules on the board. You develop a shortage of tacks and pushpins, and before you know what happened, the board is loaded with pieces of paper, one crucified on top of another, making the whole mess a vertical paper burial ground that ultimately leaves you with an obnoxiously nonfunctional eyesore.

The most obvious solution to the problem is to get rid of the thing altogether. If you think about it, you'll probably admit that what a bulletin board does is postpone the fact that you need to make a decision about a piece of paper. After all, where should you *put* that postcard and cartoon? The Clutter Checklist provides a few ideas, but for even more information about where to put the paperphernalia on your bulletin board, see also *Papers,* and check all the categories that pertain to the junk on your board. Then put it all somewhere else (your best bet — in the trash can) and take that bulletin board down. You've got enough clutter without hanging it on the wall.

Business Cards
(see also Bulletin Boards, Papers, Phone Numbers)

People hand out business cards willy-nilly, and accept them with about as much abandon. Back in the office, you start to move them from place to place in a half-hearted attempt to figure out what to actually *do* with them. Whatever you do, do not, I repeat, *do not,* put them in those plastic business card holders that hold about a zillion cards. This looks like a good system until you actually need a phone number or name from one of the business cards. Only then

✔ CLUTTER CHECKLIST

If you can't figure out what to do with the paperphernalia hanging on the board now, here's some suggestions:

❑ **Postcards** (see also *Postcards*) — Put these in a plastic shoe box and store them with other memorabilia, or better yet, throw them away.

❑ **Phone Numbers** (see also *Phone Numbers*) — Put these in a file or container of some kind to be later transferred onto a Rolodex.

❑ **Office Telephone Exchanges** — These can be put in a plastic page cover and placed under or near the telephone for quick reference.

❑ **Schedules** — Schedules, including those for sporting events, the theater season, the children's special events, and upcoming classes should be put in a file marked SCHEDULES. Put the file in the back of, or near, your desk calendar.

❑ **Tickets** — Put these in your wallet so that when you go to the event you have them, and don't have to spend a frantic twenty minutes before you rush out the door trying to remember where you put them.

do you realize that you have to thumb through all of the cards to get to the one you want, because there is no way to efficiently alphabetize the cards as they are put into the plastic sleeves. You'll be better off if you put the cards with your phone numbers and add them to your Rolodex when you can. Some cards can be trimmed with scissors along the top or bottom edge and then stapled directly onto a Rolodex card, saving you the time it would otherwise take to transfer the information. In the end, some cards aren't worth transferring to the Rolodex. These are the cards you accepted when they were offered because you didn't want to be rude. Now that nobody is looking, throw those cards away.

Calendars
(see also Announcements, Bulletin Boards)

People save calendars for lots of reasons. Some folks like the pictures, people who have ten versions of the current year are gripped by the I-really-should-keep-it syndrome, and still others keep calendars to maintain a record of appointments for tax purposes. If you have recorded business appointments or expenses on a calendar, it should be saved and filed with your tax records of the corresponding year. If that's not why you have more than one calendar, then what is the reason? I know—they're so . . . so . . . well, so *useful*—aren't they? Yes and no. One is useful. Ten is clutter. Throw them away. I'm not even going to say give them away, because in all likelihood, nobody you know wants them.

But if you are saving calendars because you like the pictures, the question of what to do with them becomes decidedly more problematic. Chances are, the calendars are perpetually buried in piles of papers and magazines, and you never even see those pretty pictures anyway. If you file them (ouch! please don't do that!), you'll never look at them again, and they'll just clutter up your files. You could frame them, but there's no telling what people will think of that.

And don't even think of putting them on a bulletin board or on the front of the refrigerator! What you can do with the pictures is to put them in albums, make a collage with them, or use them for gift wrap. These uses for calendars, especially outdated calendars, are limited, so *use it or lose it.*

Candles
(see also Holiday Decorations)

Candles are great for fancy dinners, romantic evenings, and unexpected power outages. If you don't anticipate regular fancy dinners or romantic evenings, you can probably toss or give away those half-dozen boxes of tapers that are gathering dust in the dining room buffet. Keep one box for holidays and unexpected excitement. I'm a great believer in being prepared, so it never hurts to have a sturdy candle or a couple of votives in each room in case there is a power outage. (A flashlight in each room, particularly in the bedrooms, can also be a real lifesaver.) While you don't need to keep a crate of candles on hand leftover from your hippie days, it never hurts to keep some tasteful candles to use when you need to shed a little light on a subject.

It's always a good idea to keep a small box or two of birthday candles on hand, but there's no point in keeping holiday candles in the shape of Christmas trees or Easter eggs. Those things never burn quite right anyway, and if you didn't use them during the last holiday, you probably won't use them for the next holiday either.

Canning Supplies

Glass jars, lids, and rubber seals can create chaos in an otherwise orderly kitchen cabinet. Assuming you don't can foods on a weekly or monthly basis, you should probably take all of the canning supplies out of the cabinet and drawers and put them in a box. (A transfile box that you get from the office supply store is good because it's sturdy and has handles and a lid.) Stack the boxes of canning supplies near your other home-canned goods. If you store your canned goods in the basement or in a porch pantry, put the supplies in that area. That way, next time you have a canning session, you can carry a box of supplies all at one time. You'll save the time and aggravation you used to experience carrying two or three jars at a time back and forth to the work area, and you won't have to spend your time digging endlessly to find everything you need to put up those yummies that everyone loves so much.

Even if you do have room in your kitchen (unlikely) for all of those supplies, you'll still want to consider storing them elsewhere since they're only used on a seasonal basis. You can put that kitchen cupboard space to better use for storage of items you use on a daily or weekly basis.

And by the way, if you haven't canned so much as a tomato in five years or more, maybe it's time to give up the ghost. Give all your gear to someone who does can regularly, and ask for a sample or two of the canned delights. Even if all you get is one jar of those goodies, it's one jar more than you are getting now.

Car Accessories & Supplies
(see also Maps)

Car clutter belongs as close to the car as you can get it, without (in most cases) actually putting it *in* the car. Cleaners, waxes, oil, and other handy-dandy maintenance stuff goes in the garage or carport. If you don't have cabinets or shelves in the garage, store those items in a rubber dishpan-type bin or a sturdy box with a lid (a transfile box purchased from an office supply store can do the job). If you don't have a carport or garage, this box can be stored and stacked on a closet shelf or floor (the hall closet usually serves this need).

Safety supplies, such as flares, the spare tire, and jack, obviously belong in the trunk of the car. Some people have so much other clutter in the trunk, there's no room for the spare; if this sounds like you, get rid of those papers from the office, tools, toys, pet gear, and

© Tough Tote™ Container
by Rubbermaid®

whatever else is rattling around and get that spare tire back in the car where it belongs. While most spare tires and jacks have a specific resting space in the trunk, other things, like flares, paper towels, a flashlight, rags, and extra water, do not. These traveling emergency supplies can be organized in a large canvas bag or in a sturdy box and kept in the trunk. Once you corral these supplies, you will very likely eliminate that curious clankety-clank sound that seems to emanate from the trunk whenever you hit a bump or round a corner. And you'll find that you don't have to move everything each time you add something to the trunk (like your mother-in-law's luggage or the groceries).

Cards

(see also Bulletin Boards, Gifts, Mail, Memorabilia, Papers, Postcards)

Greeting cards choke our files and bureau drawers, and otherwise invade other piles of papers on a daily basis. It starts with birth announcements and birthdays, and continues with graduations, weddings, parties, mother's and father's day, funeral announcements, sympathies, thank you's, and a host of other reason-to-send-or-receive-a-card events. You can't seem to let go of the cards you've received because the event was so memorable. Multiply this card by the number of friends and relatives who send you cards and multiply *that* by the potential number of memorable events in your life, and you're looking at a house full of cards contributing to your ongoing clutter conditions. Cards are nice to receive, and they do remind us how wonderful we are, but keeping every single greeting that you (or your children) receive can be hopelessly redundant. Select a special few from each truly *important* occasion, and store them in either albums or plastic storage boxes. Throw the rest away. And if you are saving all of the cards your children ever received, you can part with at least 80 percent of those as well. After all, if your kids don't care enough about them to figure out what to do with them, why should you take on the task?

For those of you who are always picking up greeting cards in the stores because they are so pretty, or clever, or funny—or just plain perfect for some occasion (what occasion, you don't know at this particular moment)—try to curb your card-buying habit until you send out some of the ones you already have. And, to avoid having to search for an appropriate card (you know you have one around there somewhere), try storing all of your unused cards in a nice basket with a handle. Add some stamps and a pen, and suddenly your this-calls-for-a-card obligation becomes a simple and pleasant task that can be handled at your desk, from your easy chair, or your bed.

Catalogs
(see also Desk, Magazines, Mail, Newspapers, Papers)

Once during a question and answer period of a lecture I was giving, a woman asked me how long a person should keep catalogs. Responding with my usual intellectual snap, I said, "Well, I dunno, how long do you keep yours?" "Oh," she replied, "about four seasons." I never had to say another word in answer to the question; five minutes of hysterical laughter from the audience said it all.

I think catalogs serve a terrific purpose—I've even listed super catalogs in the Resource Helpline at the back of the book. They can be a time-saving alternative to shopping that's as simple as picking up the telephone or filling out an order blank. But keeping them beyond one season—whether it's a seed catalog or a fashion catalog—is ridiculous. Prices change, and merchandise isn't kept in stock past a certain date anyway. Still, some people collect them compulsively, hopelessly adding to their mounting piles of paper, magazines, and newspapers. The people who find themselves with uncontrollable catalog clutter generally fall into one of two categories:

1. **Dreaming Before Deciding**—These people dream over catalogs, but when it comes down to the nitty-gritty, they can't decide if they want to buy anything or not. So they hold on to the catalog. Indefinitely.

   What to Do—If you're a dreamer who has trouble deciding, bite the bullet with do or die decisions. When you get a catalog, put it in your TO READ pile (see *Paper*) and then

---

✍ CLUTTER CHECKLIST

With safety equipment in the trunk, what other car clutter could there possibly be? Consider these possibilities and what to do with them:

❏ **Change** — Put change (for tolls and parking meters) in the console, and keep it there. If you don't have a recession in your console, use a plastic container of some sort. If you can, glue or in some way attach the container to the dash so you always have it within reach. If this isn't possible, get a container with a lid that at least ensures the money stays put and can be retrieved when necessary.

❏ **Documents** — The only documents you should keep in the car are those required by law — usually the registration and your insurance identification. You might also want to keep your auto club card in the car, and it's always a good idea to keep the name and phone number of your insurance agent either in your wallet or in the glove compartment.

❏ **Gym Clothes** — These either go in the trash or the washing machine, depending on how long they've been simmering in your vehicle.

❏ **Ice Scraper** — In summer, put this in the box of supplies in the trunk. In winter, keep it in the glove compartment (if it fits), or under your seat.

❏ **Makeup** (see also *Cosmetics, Handbags*) — Makeup melts into a gooey mess when left in the car, so I can't figure out why women put it there in the first place. I suppose it's so they can spend lots of time applying the stuff to their faces at red lights (which turn green before they're finished) and in parking spaces that other people are waiting for. You've probably guessed I'm against using the car as a dressing room while others wait.

---

go through it at your first opportunity. And no, the first opportunity is *not* when you are in the middle of some other distasteful chore. (People just love to stop what they're doing to look through a catalog.) You don't have to look at it right this minute, but when you do, be prepared to make a decision right then about any purchases you are going to make —

Hairbrushes and combs in the car provoke the same response from me — and these days, men often spend as much time fussing over their hair as women do. If you want to primp, retire gracefully to another room (such as the restroom) *before* you go out to the car. Keep your beauty paraphernalia in your purse if you must, but do not keep it in the car.

❏ **Maps** (see also *Maps*) — There's no need to have a map of every state sliding around with you every day. One map for the state and city you are actually *in* should do the trick. To keep it handy when traveling, try clamping it to the visor with a clothespin or putting it in a special organizer that attaches to the visor. You can also keep maps in the more obvious traditional spots, such as the glove compartment and the pocket in the door.

❏ **Sales Gear** — Sales people haul a mountain of stuff around with them, virtually operating out of their cars every day. If this is you, try keeping pens, pencils, paper clips, stapler, and the like in a small tool or tackle box. Instead of files, which tend to spill at the first abrupt stop, put some of your papers (particularly leads) in a binder; keep a hole puncher in the tool box so you can add to the binder when necessary. Also, keep a cigar box in the car for business cards and miscellaneous phone numbers. And yes, each day, spend a few minutes cleaning the car up and getting organized for the next day, just as you would if it were a desk.

❏ **Sunglasses** — Oh, all right. One pair only.

❏ **Toys** — Unless the kids are always in the car, get the toys out of the car and into the house where they belong. If the kids are always in the car, keep a small box of select toys in the trunk, to be played with during daily car travels. You can also hang a holder with pockets on the back of the front car seat to hold everything from coloring books and crayons to baby bottles or baseball cards.

or TOSS THE THING IN THE TRASH! A slightly less painful alternative is to cut out the page with the item you are going to buy, pull out the order blank and affix your mailing label from the front of the catalog, and throw the rest of the catalog away. Now, as soon as you get the money, attach it to the completed order blank and mail it off.

2. Catalog Junkies — Catalog junkies have no problem whatsoever deciding what to buy — they order something from just about every catalog that lands in their mailbox. The junkie spends an awful lot of money and time ordering things. Then the stuff comes in the mail, and invariably some of it is the wrong size or color, or it just doesn't look as good as it did in the catalog, so even more time and money gets spent to send it back. It's a habit, and an expensive one at that.

What to Do — Junkies would do well to wean themselves off their habit by not even looking at some of the catalogs that come in the mail. If you get three this week, try tossing one without even looking at it. I know you'll survive, and it'll save you money too.

Ultimately, whichever type you are, take a look at how many you are receiving each month (check that corner pile if you don't know where to begin). If you're getting more than half a dozen catalogs per quarter (yes, quarter), you are past your limit. Drop a note to some of the more useless catalog companies and let them know that you can't bear to be faced with so many options on such a regular basis, so would they kindly remove your name from their mailing list. Don't cancel the catalogs with the organizing products in them though — you're still going to need some help corralling the rest of the clutter in your life.

CHA•OS A condition of confusion and total disarray, as the original unformed state of the universe. Or, what your life has become since clutter took over.

Children
(see also Baby Clothes, Balls, Car Accessories & Supplies — Toys, *Games, Memorabilia, Sports Equipment, Stuffed Animals, Toys)*

Children, of course, are most definitely not clutter. But the clutter they generate can be mind boggling. Toys, school papers and projects, sports equipment, and clothes can often seem to take over the house, leaving (gasp!) precious little room for the more necessary adult clutter. Since nearly everyone at one time or another has had problems with the kid's clutter, and more importantly, with getting the kids to actually take care of their own stuff, the question is how to get the kids to take over their own clutter control chores. (See Clutter Checklist on pages 50 and 51.)

Start early on with the In & Out Inventory Rule. If something new comes in, something old goes out. Toys that are broken or have lost their allure can go to a charity when new toys come in the door. Teach your child the value of giving, versus the hopelessness of hoarding too many possessions.

Cleaning Supplies

I know a lot of very disorganized people who are impossible clean freaks. They have every imaginable type of exotic cleaner with special rags for this, and special rags for that. I think clean is a good thing, but I'm not willing to store a raft of cleaning supplies and gadgets that outnumbers the things I need cleaned. Keeping the supplies organized is easy if you just stock the basics.

Look for more all-purpose cleaners that will do double, or even triple, duty for you. Too often people run out and buy the latest fancy-smancy cleaner, and then it never gets used, because when it comes right down to the cleaning nitty-gritty, nobody wants to cart a zillion bottles all over the house to do something as simple as *clean.* If you've got a lot of gourmet cleaning products that you never use, give them to someone who wants to spend more of their time cleaning than you do.

If you live in a small apartment, don't overdo it with too many duplicates. One can of cleanser in the bathroom and one in the kitchen saves a lot of running back and forth, but four backup cans take up too much space. On the other hand, if you live in a two-story house, it can be a good idea to have a stash of cleaning supplies (including, if possible, an extra vacuum) on the second floor.

Let's face it, unless you were born in a barn, cleaning is something that has to be done regularly. By organizing your approach to cleaning and your cleaning supplies, you'll gain more time for yourself to be used in more interesting areas of your life. Also, once you've cleared up the rest of the clutter in your life, maintaining that clutter-free space on a regular basis contributes significantly to the overall organizational effort. In the end, cleaning is part of getting, being, and staying organized and clutter-free. (See Clutter Checklist on page 53.)

☑ CLUTTER CHECKLIST

Children will be more likely to clean up their own clutter if you provide clutter control aids that make sense to them. Try these:

❑ **Bins** — Make use of bins wherever possible, particularly for smaller children. They can be put on shelves, on the closet floor, and under the bed for easy retrieval. A sturdy dishpan can hold any number of things, including crayons, puzzle pieces, and shoes. Tossing shoes into a bin may not be the most elegant answer to the shoe organization problem, but it can help eliminate the frustrating searches for a missing sneaker when you're late for the soccer game.

❑ **Closets** — Lower rods to accommodate the child's height so that putting clothes away is a simple matter. You can raise them as the child grows.

Clocks

A clock in every corner invariably means that wherever you look, it's a different time of day. This is guaranteed to drive you buggy, especially if you are chronically late to begin with. You can simplify your life by having only one clock in your bedroom, synchronized

❑ **Clothes Hamper/Bag** — Keep a hamper or a large canvas or cotton bag in the room for dirty clothes. The bag can hang by a cord from the closet or bedroom doorknob. Kids are more likely to deposit dirty clothes if they don't have to go very far to do it.

❑ **Hooks & Pegs** — Hang hooks and pegs on the wall at the children's level. They can hang clothes, school bags, and large cotton or canvas bags for toys or school supplies.

❑ **Rolling Basket Systems** — These carts can be used to hold all manner of things, including underwear, sports clothes and equipment, and art projects and supplies (like that macaroni art that everyone holds so dear). You can also use this cart to eliminate the problem of what to do with school papers. Simply turn it into a filing cart by hanging Pendaflex files on rails (you can purchase these with the cart). Label the files Awards, Reading, Spelling, Writing, and so on. Inside each Pendaflex file, place a manila file folder with the same label. Now your children can proudly show you their daily schoolwork, and, after you have oohed and aahed over it, they can just as proudly file it in their own "filing cabinet." This system teaches and creates organization at the same time.

At the end of the school year, remove the manila file folders, sort through them with the child, and save the best. Put these in a transfile box, and mark it with your child's age and the year, and store it as you do mementos (see *Memorabilia*). Be careful not to get carried away by keeping every scrap of paper the child brings home, however. If you do, you'll need to rent a warehouse to store it all. This cart should take your child through his high school years, serving as a school records and supply center that can be rolled to the homework area as needed. When the little darling finally leaves the nest, you can use the cart yourself for clothes, projects, or hobby or stationery supplies.

with the other clocks in the house. Now, regardless of which clock you look at, you'll know exactly how late you are running.

Clocks that don't work should either be fixed and used or given to a charity that fixes things. If you can't find the time to get it repaired or to call the local charity, throw it away. After all, it's not going to wake you up tomorrow morning, is it?

Closets

*(see also Bags, Clothes, and any other category
of clutter you happen to be harboring)*

The phrase "behind closed doors" takes on a special meaning when it comes to closets. Some things get put into closets never to reemerge. Years later some hapless soul decides to organize. Junk and treasures come tumbling out to exclamations of "I can't believe it! I wondered what happened to that," and, "What on earth is *this* doing in here?"

Usually closets get cleaned out only as a last resort. When people say they have to move because they don't have enough room, what they really mean is that they don't have enough *closet* space. The choice then becomes crystal clear: clean out the closets and get rid of some stuff; or spend a fortune to move to larger, more expensive quarters. When you consider the cost of moving versus the cost of organizing, you may very well decide to do the latter.

A good starting point is the utility closet. Also known as the spare closet, the hall closet, the back closet, the front closet, and the linen closet, this is the closet that holds a cornucopia of belongings frequently suited for a time capsule. These closets provide shelter for all manner of things, including (but certainly not limited to):

Boxes of books	Linens
Boxes of receipts, dating back ten years	Paper bags
	Pet kennels, leashes
Boots	Slide projector (and eighteen carousel trays)
Broken lamps and/or small appliances	
	Spare tire
Clothes for charity	Sports gear
Coats, jackets, sweaters	Suitcases
Craft supplies	Tools
Empty boxes	Toys and games
Gift paper and ribbons	Trophies
Half-empty cans of paint	Umbrellas, some broken
Hats, gloves, scarves	Vacuum cleaner and attachments
Kitty litter	

Start by getting some large cartons and mark them:

CHARITY
CLEANERS
TRASH
ELSEWHERE (things that go in another room)

☑ CLUTTER CHECKLIST

Traditionally, people tend to stuff cleaning supplies either under the sink, or in the pantry. You can keep the supplies and equipment neater by using some simple storage aids:

Under the Sink:

❑ **Dishpan** — This can be used to hold supplies and/or rags, and at least serves to keep everything together.

❑ **Roll-Out Basket** — These are made of sturdy wire and mount on runners under the sink so that you can pull them out and have easy access to the supplies. These baskets help cut down on the problem of bottles and cans falling over on top of each other as you reach for one in the very back of the cabinet.

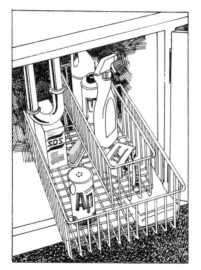

❑ **Supply Caddy** — This divided bin has a handle so that you can pick it up and carry it from room to room when you're cleaning. It's easy to store under the sink or on the pantry floor.

In the Pantry:

❑ **Door Rack** — You can install a door rack with shelves that mounts on the inside of the door — which is otherwise usually overlooked as potential storage space.

❑ **Strip Rack** — For mops and brooms, a strip rack with pressurized grooves or loops can be installed on the inside wall of your pantry to keep all the equipment orderly and up off the floor.

Then pull *everything* out of the closet, sorting as you go. If something needs to be cleaned or altered, put it in the appropriate box. Things that go in another room include toys and games (put these in the kids' rooms), old Tupperware® and sets of dishes (into the kitchen, dining room, or charity box with this stuff), and books, magazines, and newspapers (see also *Books, Magazines, and Newspapers*).

You can reduce the avalanche of linens by putting a fresh set of linens in each bedroom (see also *Linens*). Placemats that you haven't used in five years can go to charity or to your sister. Linens with impossible stains could be turned into rags for cleaning. You can put sports gear in a big garbage can in the garage (see also *Sports Equipment*), and papers that are more than ten years old should hit the trash can without remorse. Coats, jackets, and boots that you never wear definitely go to charity, and any other clothes should be in good repair and clean. Only put back items that you regularly use. To get rid of the rest of the stuff, ask yourself how often you use it, and if you'd be willing to pay to move it.

When you've finished, distribute the contents of the boxes. Put the things that go in other rooms in those rooms. Then go straight to the car with the items for charity, the cleaners, and the tailor and drop the items off at the appropriate place. If the boxes sit around the house for any length of time, both you and members of your family will start pulling things *out* of the boxes. The trash box and the charity box, in particular, invite wails of anguish as family members insist that you can't possibly be getting rid of this or that treasure. Before you know it, the stuff will be all over the place again, and in an effort to neaten up the clutter, you'll put it right back where it doesn't belong—in the closet.

Clothes
(see also Baby Clothes, Handbags, Hats, Jewelry, Laundry, Shoes & Boots, Socks & Stockings, Ties, Uniforms)

When some people get up in the morning, their feet hit the floor running. They skid over to the crammed closet and hastily extract an outfit. But this makes them even more frantic, because now the garment has to be ironed, since the closet is in such a mess that everything always has to be pressed before it can be worn. For these people, the ironing board never gets put away.

> **PITCH** To project from the hand in a forward, thrusting motion; fling; throw; hurl at something. Or, what you should probably do with at least 50 percent of your clutter, but what you won't do because you'll fall back on the Pack Rat's Excuse Almanac.

Clothes closets represent a killer closet category that often defies description. The word "crammed" is usually an understatement. Evening clothes, sporting clothes, work clothes, play clothes, old clothes, new clothes, and even dirty clothes, all vie for the precious little space allowed by the average closet. Hangers get tangled up with plastic cleaner bags and with each other, and accessories such as belts and ties either fall on the floor or get caught in the middle of the rest of the mess. One day, I'm convinced I'll pick up the newspaper to see headlines screaming about "The Closet That Ate New York." To insure that your closet doesn't wind up in the day's headlines, you can tackle the problem head-on.

First, pull everything out of the closet. (Once you have everything scattered all over the room, you have reached a level of commitment that will only be relieved when you can see the bed that is now buried under a ton of clothes.)

Set up special cartons for sorting your clothes as you go through them. You'll want cartons marked CHARITY, TRASH, OTHER ROOM, and MENDING/ALTERATIONS. Tackle the mountain of clothes one garment at a time, giving each item careful consideration; does it really go back in the closet or does it belong in a carton? A word of warning here: the MENDING/ALTERATIONS carton is not supposed to be a holding bin that sits around indefinitely. Take those clothes to the seamstress *immediately*. Don't even consider doing them yourself. If those clothes have been waiting to be mended for months already—and you haven't done it because you haven't had the time—you're not going to do it now. So put that box filled with mendings and alterations in the car at the end of your organizing session, along with the charity box, and drop both of them off without delay.

If at all possible, I recommend having a friend help you clean out your clothes closet. This friend should be selected with care. You'll want a person who will criticize your taste and doesn't mind adding some tongue clucking. That way, when you hold up that miniskirt that looked great fifteen years and twenty pounds ago, your friend's uncontrolled giggles will answer the question of what to do with it once and for all.

Things that you know are the wrong color or "just not you" should go to charity. Other avenues of giving are resale shops, and by golly, that friend who sits there and tells you how silly it looks on you might just take the garment herself. The important thing is to get everything inappropriate *out of the closet and out of the house,* so you won't be tempted to put it back in the closet "for now."

Things that are too small (and have been for quite some time), out of date, or that been been waiting to be altered for just about forever, should also be given away. If it's way too big or you never really liked it in the first place, get rid of it.

As you're deciding which clothes to keep, watch out for that many-tentacled monster, the *I can't get rid of this* syndrome:

- **"I can't get rid of this!** As soon as I lose twenty-five pounds, I'll be able to wear it again." If you can lose twenty-five pounds, you deserve a whole new wardrobe. *Get rid of it!*
- **"I can't get rid of this** because if I hold onto it long enough, it'll come back in style." Even if it *does* come back in style, you can bet designers will do an updated version and you'll feel slightly off-center wearing it. *Get rid of it!*
- **"I can't get rid of this** — I paid too much money for it!" (Or *them* if you're talking about shoes.) If you paid too much money for something, whose fault is that? Furthermore, do you want to continue to spend money in the form of storage space (square footage costs money, remember)? *Get rid of it!*
- **"I can't get rid of this** because it's so *good* — I'm saving it for a special occasion." Every day is a special occasion, so unless it's covered with sequins and bugle beads and cut clear down to your navel, either use it or lose it.

Another stumbling block to cleaning out the closet is the *Whens:*

- **"When** I get something to go with this, I'll wear it." Oh? And *when* might that be, and how long have you been saying that?
- **"When** I get this altered, it will be fine." So get it altered. Right now.
- **"When** my husband takes me out (admittedly not that often), he likes me to wear these shoes — he thinks they look sexy. Otherwise I don't wear them, because they kill my feet and hurt by back." Let me see now, does this mean that they *don't*

hurt your feet and kill your back when your husband takes you out? Get rid of them, or give them to your husband, and let him dance down the driveway in them!

As you put good clothes back in the closet, aim for a simple wardrobe that is comfortable, attractive, and interchangeable. Only keep the clothes that you feel good about wearing. Get rid of any wire hangers and put your clothes on good plastic hangers or skirt and/or pant hangers.

Plastic hangers are better than wire hangers for more than one reason. You can easily hang all of your clothes facing in the same direction, and believe it or not, this makes the clothes in the closet hang neater and saves space. (Regardless of how you hang the garment on the hanger, all you need to do is swivel the head of the hanger to make it face in the right direction). Since plastic hangers are thicker than wire ones, your clothes are less likely to get smashed and crushed. Plastic hangers also have notches to hang straps of gowns and thin strapped blouses so that they won't fall off, and plastic hangers stay cleaner than wire hangers, which are natural dust collectors. Finally, everyone has experienced, at one time or another, the frustration of tangled wire hangers — plastic hangers put an end to that annoyance.

Don't leave plastic (from the cleaners) on the garments. It only makes the garment difficult to see, and is dangerous for children

and pets. If you are hanging on to these plastic shrouds to keep
dust off clothes, ask yourself why the garment is collecting dust.

Group the clothes you wear in categories:

PANTS	ATHLETIC CLOTHES
SKIRTS	DRESSY CLOTHES
TOPS	LINGERIE
SHIRTS	SWEATERS (if you hang
DRESSES	them)
SUITS	SHOES
JACKETS	ACCESSORIES

Hang the categories grouped by color. This makes selecting
and coordinating outfits much quicker and easier. Make sure you
place the hangers facing the same way—this really does save
space. Empty hangers can be put at the end of the rod so you
know where they are, stored in another closet, or placed on an
extra rod that you can install about six inches from the closet top
shelf. (To organize your footwear, see *Shoes & Boots*.)

It helps to put accessories such as ties, belts, scarves, hats, and
handbags in an easily accessible area of the closet or in your dressing area. (See also *Ties, Handbags,* and *Hats*) You can install one
of several different types of closet organizational aids to help
accessories and other articles of clothing organized within the
closet.

You may also want to install a double rod system, which effectively doubles the available closet space by putting one rod up
over another, measured so that blouses and shirts can hang on
the top rod, and pants or skirts can be hung on the rod below.
While the top rod is a bit higher than a normal single rod system,
it is reachable, and makes selecting and coordinating outfits a
simple matter and takes up a minimum of closet space.

Or you may want to call in a closet company to put in a new
closet interior. Often these companies can double and even triple
your closet space by adding shelves, rods, and basket systems.

Other Clothes

Clothes not stored in closets can include underwear, sleepwear, socks and stockings, T-shirts, sweatshirts, and sweaters.
These clothes should be gone through as ruthlessly as you go
through your closet—get rid of everything that doesn't fit, is the
wrong color, is stupid (like some of those T-shirts with those ridic-

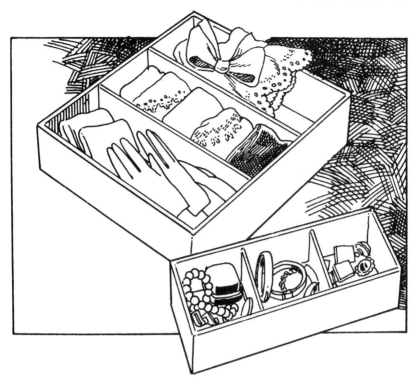

ulous statements that you once thought were so profound), and/ or is out of date. Underwear with hopelessly stretched-out elastic or stains can become rags. Socks without mates can go — hanging on to one sock past sixty days or so is like clinging to a fantasy. That other sock is not going to miraculously reappear, so give it up. Check that pile of stockings and pantyhose for runs, and get rid of all but the unblemished pairs. Resist the temptation to save more than a few "work clothes" for when you "work" in the garden or on the car. You don't need a complete wardrobe for those activities. A couple of pairs of old pants and a few T-shirts or sweatshirts will do the trick. Tennis clothes and ski gear should be checked for fit and condition. Along with things that don't fit, get rid of any stained or ripped clothes that you don't wear.

Accessories, such as scarves, belts, and gloves, should also be checked for fit and appropriateness. Belt styles change right along with waist measurements, so get rid of the ones that don't fit or are out of style. Pretty scarves tend to get put in a drawer and forgotten; go through these, remind yourself of how pretty they are, make a note of how you can wear them with your current clothes, and then do just that—*wear them.* Otherwise, give them to friends or to charity. Gloves are always useful if you *wear* them,

☑️ CLUTTER CHECKLIST

Once you have cleaned out your closet and/or installed a new space saving system, you should resolve to keep the closet stocked only with appropriate clothing that you wear frequently and enjoy thoroughly. To avoid making shopping mistakes in the future, shop with these guidelines in mind:

❑ **Inventory** — Make an inventory of what you already have. Then sit down and make a list of what you *need* — not what you *want*. If you have a tailored skirt you never wear because you need a certain type of blouse to go with it, then you *need* that blouse. On the other hand, if you just saw an ad for a fabulous pair of sequined dress pumps and you almost *never* go out to dressy affairs, although you may *want* those pumps, you probably don't *need* them. (Your black patents will do beautifully.)

❑ **Don't Leave Home Without It** — Take your list with you, and don't buy anything that isn't on the list, no matter what.

❑ **Make Color Work for You** — Determine what your best colors are, and then stick to that color palette. Try to keep it to four basic colors or less, and don't allow yourself to be suckered into buying something in this season's newest, faddiest color, when you know perfectly well it doesn't look good on you. If your colors mix well, the number of mix-and-match outfits at your disposal increases substantially.

❑ **Coordinate Outfits** — Wear your favorite blouse, shirt, or blazer when you shop — or bring it with you. You can buy pieces to work with it, and you can mix and match as you go.

❑ **Classics Count** — Classic, well-made clothes are worth the price. You can wear them for years, and always look terrific.

---

but like socks, if one is missing, the other one is worthless. No sense spending the next three winters with that one glove mingling with the pairs you have in the bureau. Handbags can be hung on pegs, hooks, or a mug rack, or they can be stored on shelves with vertical dividers (make them by having pieces of plywood cut to fit) to keep the bags stored upright.

Drawers can be better organized by placing dividers and other organizers into the drawer. This can be as simple as putting shoe boxes in a drawer to separate socks and stockings, or you can

❑ **Cozy Up** — Make friends with a salesperson or personal shopper (on staff at the better department and specialty stores) and make sure they know your taste in clothes, color preferences, and sizes, as well as what you might need in the way of outfits and/or accessories.

❑ **Shop Spring & Fall** — Try shopping twice a year only. Depending on your budget, this may mean that as soon as the fall fashions come out you do your shopping, and when the new summer styles come out, you shop again. If your pocketbook can't handle those full prices, you can still shop twice each year, except instead of running out to shop the minute the new fashions are presented, wait until they go on sale; then go out and make your purchases. Just before summer fashions are introduced, the winter things go on sale, and that's the time to buy your winter clothes. When the new winter styles are about to be presented, all of the spring and summer things go on sale. That's the time to buy your summer clothes. Generally, if you shop wisely, you'll find that your clothing purchases won't be out of synch with the styles, partly because the fashion industry shows things well before we are ready for them. Winter things come out in July when it's hotter than blazes and go on sale sometime between November and January when you are freezing your watzit off, which can make sale time the time to buy for more reasons than one.

❑ **Shop Sales Carefully** — Don't buy something just because it is on sale. If you don't need it, what difference does it make if it's on sale? On the other hand, if it's on sale, and it's on your list, snap it up, and take it home and brag your brains out to everyone within earshot about what a great bargain you got.

order custom dividers to hold your lingerie and/or jewelry. Rolling basket systems can replace dressers, or add to them by providing extra storage space (you can roll them directly into your closet if you like). Some things stay neater longer if they are put on a shelf rather than in a drawer. T-shirts and sweaters, for instance, seem to do better on a shelf where you can see at a glance what's there and pull out what you need. A drawer invites rummaging to get at what lies on the bottom. Once you've done some digging in a drawer, there is usually very little motivation (or time) to put things back in order. Somehow a shelf is easier to keep neater, especially if you install dividers (you can get plastic ones that snap into place to keep the stacks neater). If you do move items to a shelf from the drawer, don't make the stacks too high, or you'll have collapsing piles of clothing all over the place.

You can also make use of stackable see-through sweater and lingerie boxes as well as under-bed storage drawers for storing out of season clothes, thus freeing up drawer space for the clothes that you're wearing now. Cedar chests, wicker trunks, and vinyl storage units will also provide storage space for out-of-season clothes.

Whatever methods and storage equipment you use for your clothes, keep your wardrobe current by weeding out inappropriate clothes as you go. If you start losing control over the closet, remember the In & Out Inventory Rule—something new comes in, something old goes out. It works every time.

Collections

(see also Antiques, Baskets, Hats, Knickknacks, Memorabilia, Photographs, Postcards, Rocks, Salt & Pepper Sets, Souvenirs, Stuffed Animals)

Collections can definitely be hazardous to your organizational health. Whether it's license plates or butterflies, collections start with interest and end in out-of-control clutter. You may even be like Pat the Pack Rat, who collected *everything* for no particularly rational reason. Like her cat's whiskers, which she said were magical. When they fell off his face, she saved 'em, and the only reason she didn't have a *huge* collection of whiskers was that the cat didn't shed his whiskers all that often. So unless what you're collecting is appreciating at a dollar rate that exceeds the cost of the square footage needed to house it (such as antiques), or unless your collection gives you pleasure on a daily basis, you would do well to pass it on to someone else or pitch it.

Collections from your childhood days that are now stored in the garage do not actively contribute to your general health and welfare. Collections that are stored all over the house, both in full view and behind cupboard doors and in drawers, require dusting and moving around every time you need more space for something else. If you can't bear getting rid of the entire collection, keep a small precious selection, and get rid of the rest. And if you have children who are beginning to shift into the collector's mode, set firm limits now, before it gets out of hand. Otherwise you'll have rocks, stickers, and who knows what all, all over the house. They can cull their collection by selecting only the most important items. This will teach them the value of organization, space utilization, and it will help them prioritize the accumulation of things in their lives. Whatever is chosen can be displayed in albums, as a collage, on a bookcase or in a cabinet. Keep the collection confined to that particular space allocation by using the In & Out Inventory Rule.

After you have taken the steps necessary to cut back on your collection, a little preventative maintenance is in order. Make sure you announce to family, friends, and associates, that you are no longer collecting, so that they can stop aiding and abetting your collection clutter by giving you gifts to add to your habit. And the next time you pass a beautiful porcelain frog (if frogs are your thing) or a fantastic rock (rock hounds relate to this), close your eyes and pass it by. Eventually, you won't even think about, or miss, that collection.

College Papers
(see also Papers)

Dusty college papers always make me think of school, and school makes me think of tests. So, for those of you who feel you must keep those college papers, here's a test for you to help you really get in the spirit of things:

1. *How* many years have you been holding onto those papers?
____ 2 or less ____ 2-5 years ____ 5-10 years
____ more than 10 years

2. *Why* are you keeping them?
____ My terrific grades serve as a testament to my unparalleled intelligence.
____ I might need them for reference some day.
____ My English Lit papers remind me that I was voted the class clown for three years in a row.

3. *Where* are these papers stored, and how much square footage do they occupy?

4. Now (here's a little math for you) multiply the square footage by the cost of that space, and write in the total dollar amount below:

5. Have the bugs found your precious papers yet? (Note: if they haven't, it's only a matter of time until they do.)

SCORING: There is no scoring system for this quiz. There is almost no way to pass this particular test, since I know of no earthly reason to save college papers (and/or textbooks).

Your class clown days are over and if you acted like that today you'd be hooted out of the community. While you may have been intelligent at some point, your intelligence is taking a beating here because it's just plain goofy to keep things like this that you never refer to or use.

If you are convinced that you'll need them for reference, I'd like to remind you that times change, for goodness sakes, and reference materials become outdated practically every other minute. Libraries can provide all of the reference you will ever need, and in all likelihood, we're talking about a trip to the library once every five or six years anyway, which is a much more sensible approach to the issue of reference. You won't need these papers someday, they do not constitute legitimate memorabilia, and they are taking up too much space and drawing bugs in the process. Let go of the past by letting go of these papers.

Cosmetics
(see also Bathroom Clutter, Handbags)

My views on cosmetics are fairly controversial. I happen to think that they do not make women beautiful. Since I stand virtually alone in this conception, I will endeavor to address the issue of cosmetics storage in a more realistic vein. Most women (and men, for that matter) do like the effects of makeup, and therefore, women buy the stuff by the truckload. But men start to wonder about the value of cosmetics when the clutter overruns anything that he hoped to store in the bathroom (such as a razor and a can of shaving cream). Men get a little bewildered about it all. Surprisingly, they don't say much about the fact that they dislike not having any bathroom space. But *I* hear it at my seminars. They don't know what to do about the cosmetic problem, which is perceived as a woman's problem (even though the women very often use cosmetics to please men). So, a word to the wise here should be sufficient; cosmetic clutter *is* noticed, and is not necessarily approved of.

The first thing to do is to go through all makeup and get rid of anything that is old, sticky, melted, or otherwise too gooey for words. Throw away hardened nail polish and mascara wands that have turned to tar. Rouges and lipsticks that you never use should go also. Face creams that look like a miniature dried-up riverbed can also be tossed. Besides the utter uselessness of old cosmetics, it is important to remember that bacteria do grow in these items, so you wouldn't want to use very old makeup anyway. Teeny tiny samples that have accumulated can either be tossed or given to charities (who are always looking for unused hygiene items for their clients). Ditto those tiny bars of soaps and shampoos that you carted home from the last hotel you stayed in. Use it or lose it. (Charities love those unused items too.)

Once you have weeded out the cosmetics, the next step is to organize what is left, and, if appropriate, reallocate the bathroom space so that it is more evenly shared. You could, for example, move your hair brushes to a bedroom spot or even to a corner in the hall outside the bathroom. Put a small stand there and keep your hair paraphernalia in the drawer to keep it handy. Hang an attractive mirror on the wall, and you've actually "extended" your bathroom.

☑ CLUTTER CHECKLIST

You can organize your cosmetics with the help of a few simple gadgets and techniques:

❑ **Makeup Center** — Use small baskets or plastic or Lucite containers to hold and group small items such as makeup brushes and manicure equipment. You'll save time because you won't have to dig for the small items, and you'll end up using less space overall as well.

❑ **Bag It** — Keep the cosmetics that you use on a regular basis in a clear plastic zippered bag. The bag can be stored out of sight in a drawer, cabinet, or covered basket. With everything in one bag, there's no searching through drawers for the lipstick. Put everything back in the bag immediately after using, and you'll be guaranteed a simple, time-saving start every day when you "put on your face." When you travel, simply grab the bag and go.

❑ **Tackle or Art Supply Box** — These portable storage units can hold and carry all manner of cosmetics and can be transported and stored easily.

❑ **Drawer Dividers** — Drawer dividers can separate and organize your cosmetics, and if you get the plastic dividers that snap together to hold cutlery, it is easy to keep them clean. Just pull out the divider that is dirty and give it a quick wash. (These dividers are also good hidden storage slots for your toothbrush and toothpaste.)

Colognes can also be applied in the bedroom, and extra supplies such as shampoos and soaps can be stored in the linen closet.

Once you've organized the cosmetic clutter, remember to periodically eliminate old bacteria-laden items, and, if at all possible, try to resist buying a new shade of this or that every time you breeze through the drugstore. When you go to the department store, bypass those cosmetic counters where dozens of beautifully made-up salespeople are just waiting to snooker you into buying yet another jar of overpriced miracle cream and racy red rouge. I personally doubt you need that stuff anyway.

Craft Supplies
(see also Art & Art Supplies, Paint & Paintbrushes, Sewing Supplies)

Craft supplies generate hard-to-store clutter that can quickly turn into a nightmare. Once the clutter takes over, the prospect of working on the craft seems to lose its magic, with unfinished projects sitting forlornly in corners, boxes, bags, and drawers. Working on too many craft projects is asking for trouble, so the first step is to

---

☑️ CLUTTER CHECKLIST

Adapt some of these storage and organizational ideas for important craft supplies:

❑ **Roll With It** — Use rolling baskets to hold the supplies and unfinished projects. When you're ready to work, simply pull the rolling basket over to your work area.

❑ **Miniatures Mastery** — Use metal parts cabinets or tool or tackle boxes to hold small items. Label each drawer for simple storage.

❑ **Can It** — Use oatmeal cartons or coffee cans to hold supplies such as knitting needles and special brushes.

❑ **Carry-all** — Use a supply caddy to hold supplies that can be easily carried to the work area. Or use wicker baskets with handles and/or covers to hold and transport supplies.

❑ **Containment** — Use bins, dishpans, and cat litter pans to hold supplies.

❑ **Divide and Conquer** — Use drawer dividers to separate supplies stored in drawers.

---

reduce the amount of supplies on hand along with the unfinished projects by eliminating all but the most necessary or fun craft paraphernalia.

If you can, set up a craft corner, and keep everything in that area. Allocate a special cabinet or chest to keep everything in, or put up shelves over a desk or table and chair to consolidate your supplies in one area. Once you've organized your supplies, set aside some time on a regular basis to clean up craft clutter by finishing projects before you start new ones. Completed handicrafts can make lovely gifts or additions to your own home or office, so what are you waiting for? Get organized, and get back to work!

Desk
(see also Announcements, Brochures, Catalogs,
Files & Filing Cabinets, Furniture, Mail, Magazines, Notes,
Papers, Pens & Pencils, Postcards)

Believe it or not, how you handle the clutter that accumulates on your desk can make or break you. Think about it. When was the last time you walked into a CEO's office to find that person sitting behind piles of desktop clutter? Although some people achieve success in spite of their clutter, they are the exception rather than the rule.

The fact is, desk clutter creates confusion and stress, cuts down significantly on personal productivity, and sets the scene for others to make a snap judgment about your capability to stay in control and get the job done. This holds true whether your desk is located in a major corporation or in the kitchen. If you can't control the clutter, chances are you can't control the job to be done, and the people who are privy to the chaos on your desk are definitely forming opinions about your overall capabilities.

The same organizing principles apply to both the home and the office. Whether you are buying equipment and supplies for your home office, or requisitioning them for your office, you'll want to get functional equipment that can handle all of your needs—from personalized stationery to hundreds of files that need to be organized and stored.

To organize your desk work area, first remove everything from the desk. Next, replace the items using some basic principles that will not only help you organize the desk, but help you *keep* it organized. As you clear the desk, you'll find that at any given time, your desk (and desktop) provides a home to the following items:

1. Equipment

2. Mail — Incoming & Outgoing

3. Papers & Files

4. Personal Items

5. Supplies

Nearly all of those categories can be accommodated in the average desk without turning to clutter. As you organize your desk, keep these organizational ideas and principles in mind:

1. **Equipment** — This includes the telephone, answering machine, typewriter, adding machine, computer, and/or any other equipment that you use on a daily basis in your work. The equipment that stays on your desk at all times should be placed so that it's within easy reach, and so it doesn't clutter the work space of your desk. If you are right-handed, place the telephone and adding machine (if you use one) to the right. Typewriters and computer equipment should be on a stand or return table either to the side of your desk or behind you, so that you have a separate work space for those typing and/or computer-related projects. You should be able to reach this work area simply by swiveling your chair around to that position at the side or behind your desk.

2. **Mail** — All too often the incoming mail buries the outgoing mail, resulting in bills being paid late and important correspondence being lost amidst the piles of paper on the desk. To reduce these potential hazards, have a specific place for incoming mail until you get around to dealing with it. Make sure nothing else gets piled on that spot.

    For outgoing mail, you might want to set up a "to go" table or spot. Put this table next to the door, and as you get mail ready to go, put it there. Then when you leave, take it with you. If there is no room or there's already furniture by the door, carve out a "to go" spot by putting a basket next to the door either on the floor or on top of the furniture that's already there. A bookcase can hold a "to go" section if you put a basket on a shelf next to the door, or you can put a red folder marked OUT on the shelf (you can stand it up on a small Lucite or plastic letter holder).

For people who rely on others to pick up and deliver mail to their office, training tags can be a lifesaver. Instead of an unmarked in and out box, try marking them with index cards. IN ONLY and OUT ONLY, in large letters affixed to the appropriate box, can help eliminate the confusion that arises when new people are assigned the task of your in and out pickups and deliveries. Even here, I believe moving the out box off the desk can be helpful. You might have to take a step to get to it, or reach it with a mighty stretch, but in addition to the exercise, you can benefit from a greater sense of order and less clutter on the top of your desk.

Once the mail arrives, of course, the real key to keeping control of the mail clutter is to open and sort it immediately. For more information on this bit of organizational wisdom, see *Mail.*

3. **Papers & Files** — The piles of papers and files that clutter desks are theoretically those you are working on at that particular time. The reality often is that among those papers and files are items that need to be filed, tossed, or put in an envelope and sent out. Magazines, newspapers, and trade journals can add to the mess, and before you know it, the top of the desk has vanished. Actually accomplishing anything is just about impossible, because you're overwhelmed from the minute you walk through the door.

There are essentially only four things to be done with the paper and files on the top of your desk. Set up these four baskets:

TO DO	**TO FILE**
TO PAY	**TO READ**

Then, of course, there's the *trash basket.*

Since your TO DO and your TO PAY baskets will be on top of your desk, use the wire ones that can be stacked. You can see into them, so you always know how much work is there, and there's plenty of room to reach in and grab the papers. Fancy smoke-colored plastic boxes that, when stacked, are impossible to work with easily, are paper traps. You can't really see what's in there, and the boxes tend to topple over, or serve as a towering dumping ground for everything you'd rather not deal with.

For your TO READ items, get a sturdy *large* wicker basket

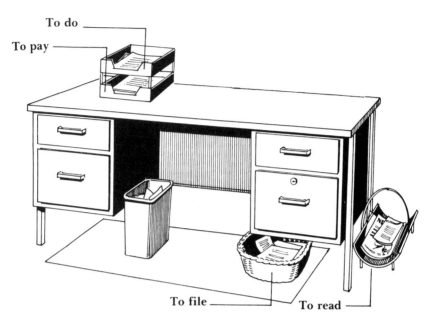

with a handle. This can be kept anywhere — on the floor next to the desk or by the credenza. At home, it's portable — you can carry it with you from room to room as needed.

For your TO FILE category, get a very roomy wicker or wire basket and put it *under* your desk. Simply toss papers and files that need to be filed into this basket, and you'll eliminate a good portion of the paper clutter that you keep moving around on the top of your desk.

For people who have ongoing projects with lots of paper-work accumulating, another option is the PROJECT or ON-GOING desktop filing system. Purchase either a graduated-step file holder or a desktop hanging file holder and put it on your desk to hold vital ongoing activities or projects; or you can set these same files up in your desk file drawer. When the project is completed, or for some reason ceases to be ongoing, simply remove the file from the desk drawer or desktop holder and return it to the permanent files. Examples of ONGOING folders might be:

> To Be Copied
> Errands to Do
> Calls to Make
> Take Home/Office
> Future Meetings (Agenda Items & Backup)
> Future Travel (Tickets, Itinerary, etc.)

Examples of PROJECT FILES might be:

> Annual Report
> Johnson Court Case
> Remodeling
> XYZ Account

A graduated-step file system of ongoing items (placed either on your desktop or on a credenza next to the desk), along with immediate project files in the desk drawer, can keep everything categorized and at your fingertips. This, along with the TO DO, TO PAY, TO FILE, and TO READ baskets, should virtually eliminate *all* of the paper and file clutter from the top of your desk.

4. **Personal Items**—Personal items that accumulate on and in desks include photographs of children and pets, paperweights, aspirin, jewelry, cash, executive toys, keys, awards, teabags, joke statues and plaques, ink-covered plastic forks, antacid tablets, nail polish, and plants. Set aside a small area in one of the drawers for personal items such as aspirin, change, and so forth, and limit yourself to that area only for those belongings. A photo or two and a plant can be acceptable on top of, or near the desk, but beyond that you are courting clutter. Unless you've got table and desktop space to spare, personal items are best kept to a minimum.

5. **Supplies**—Supplies that lurk around a desk run the gamut from stationery and envelopes to paper clips and pens (many of which don't work). Also mingled in the mess are rubber bands, stamps, ink pads, business cards, and typing and computer supplies. Round up all of the supplies and get rid of everything that's outdated or doesn't work. Old address stickers, stamps, and stationery that you don't want or use should be tossed. Get a container of some kind and put a supply of *working* pens and pencils in it. Place this on top of the desk. Toss any pens or pencils that don't work or are broken. Get a container for paper clips as well. Some containers have a magnetic top, so that clips come out singly and won't spill all over the place. A spare box of clips in the desk drawer is fine, but if you've got twenty-four boxes that you bought on sale, they should go in a storage cabinet with other office supplies. Keep the basics at hand—scissors, sta-

pler, staple remover, tape, and, if you use it, hole puncher. Everything else should be pared down to just what you use on a daily basis. Typing, computer, and other paper supplies should be kept at hand, but a gross of any one item in your desk is not necessary. One box of anything if it's small (such as clips or rubber bands), and about a fourth of a box of anything if it's large (such as stationery or envelopes) is more than enough to keep in and around your desk.

You can buy a stationery rack to hold paper and envelopes. Generally there are enough compartments to also accommodate forms that you use with regularity, and these metal holders sit easily on a desk corner or credenza for easy access whenever you need stationery or forms.

Another solution is to keep forms and paper supplies in the desk file drawer in hanging file folders. You can put these files in back of your project files in the drawer, or, if you have no project files, you can use the drawer just for these paper supplies.

Inside smaller desk drawers, you might put divider trays to help keep the small, miscellaneous supplies in some kind of order. The next time you are on the phone with some long-winded bore, open one of those drawers. In the ten minutes that you have to spend listening to Mr. or Mrs. Boring, you can tidy up an entire supply drawer.

Once your desk is organized, you'll want to keep it that way. Resist the temptation to fall back into old habits by automatically spreading papers and files all over the desk. Only put in front of you what you are working on *at that time.* Put everything else in its proper basket or ongoing or project file. Every day, before you leave your desk, spend ten to fifteen minutes putting everything away. Then put the most important piece of work in the center of your desk. When you come back to your desk the next day, you won't be greeted with mountains of clutter, and your most important work will be right in front of you.

Dishes

(see also Heirlooms, Kitchen Utensils, Pots & Pans,
Salt & Pepper Sets, Vases)

Many people have enough dishes lurking behind cabinet and hutch doors to outfit an army. There are the everyday dishes, the good dishes, the souvenir dishes, and the promotional dishes (such as the mug you got from the gas station when you filled up three times last week). Before you tackle organizing *all* of your dishes and glassware, stop and count noses in your family. If there are four people who normally eat meals at you house, two complete sets of dishes for twelve, thirty-six assorted glasses, and who knows how many mugs, are definitely more than you need. Select one set of dishes to use every day and weed out the souvenir and promotional glasses and cups (give them away) so that the dishes you use on a daily basis are accessible.

Good dishes should be reevaluated. Do you *ever* use them? Are you keeping them because you got them for your wedding (to your first husband) twenty-two years ago? Or, do you use them on major holidays only? If you *never* use them, don't wait for your death, after which they will be bequeathed to someone or left for everyone to fight over — so the winner can store them. Take the good dishes out of the cabinet now, and give them to the relative of your choice. These days, many young couples don't have lovely china, and chances are such a couple would be delighted to use your dishes for their holiday festivities. If you *do* use them yourself on holidays, you can store them on higher shelves, since you don't need to get to them on a regular basis. You can double the space of any one high shelf by adding another shelf (look for an add-a-shelf at your local variety or closet store) or by placing a plate rack on the shelf. Cups can be hung on hooks to save space, but if you want to spare yourself the chore of washing all of the good dishes before you use them, your best bet is to store them in quilted or plastic dish caddies inside the cupboard or hutch.

If you do use your good dishes frequently and have them stored in a buffet or sideboard in the dining room, chances are you are making the best use of that space. But if you don't use them (as in, almost never), you might want to reevaluate all that cabinet space. A buffet or sideboard can also accommodate cassette tapes, photographs, and craft or office supplies, among other things.

However you store your good dishes, I can't think of any reason to have more than one set of good dishes and one set of everyday dishes. If you serve more than twelve on the holidays — and find yourself using more than one set of dishes — chances are that they won't match. So if they're not going to match anyway, why not use everyday dishes at the children's places? I suppose every perfect mother, wife, and hostess, along with Miss Manners, would have my head for saying that, but I just can't see allocating extra storage space (that often doesn't exist in the first place) just so two or more sets of good dishes can be stored, only to be used once or twice each year. You have to live with your own hostess duties, so you'll have to decide this one for yourself.

And, oh yes, about those *dirty dishes.* Wash 'em and put 'em away. Yes, every day.

DIS•OR•DER The situation characterized by disarrangement; hence, inattention or neglect of orderliness. Or, that mess you've got all over the place.

Electrical Supplies
(see also Batteries, Hardware, Junk Drawer, Tools)

Electrical supplies invariably end up in that horror known as the junk drawer. Extension cords and plugs become hopelessly tangled up with the other contents of the drawer—coupons, screws and nails, matches, gloves, picture hangers, glue, spackling paste, pennies, flower seeds and bulbs, and small tools. You'll want to clean this drawer out altogether, of course, but in the meantime, you can pull out the connectors, adapters, fuses, batteries, and sockets and straighten them out so that when you need an extension cord or a plug you can actually *get* one. Extension cords can be loosely looped and put inside empty paper towel cardboard holders—keeping each one separate and tangle-free. Cords can also be looped over a hook or nail in the broom closet or in another supply storage area. Plugs and other small electrical supplies fit nicely in a clearly labeled cigar box. The box and cords can then either be put on a shelf, or, if you must, back in the junk drawer, where they will at least be organized.

Exercise Equipment
(see also Balls, Sports Equipment)

If ever there was a case for *use it, or lose it,* this is it. If you decide to use it, there's no point in trying to put it away and get it out after each use—be it barbells or an exercise bike—because if you have to fuss, you won't get it out and put it back again tomorrow. The best you can do is to allocate a room or a corner of a room and keep all of the equipment in that area, so you can just walk over to your "gym" and start exercising without worrying about pulling out (and putting back) your equipment. Don't think of the equipment as an eyesore, think of it as a daily personal achievement. I'll guarantee you that people who see it won't stop to think about how it clutters up the room. They'll be too busy thinking that they really should be exercising themselves.

Eyeglasses

Generally speaking, a spare pair of glasses is a very good idea. More than one spare pair, however, contributes to the clutter problem. When people buy new, more fashionable, or upgraded (prescription) glasses, the tendency is to hang onto the old pair. When you find yourself hanging onto a half-dozen or more pairs of eyeglasses, it's time to eliminate some of them. It seems a shame to throw away perfectly good glasses — outdated or not — and it is, but keeping them to clutter up your dresser drawer is a shame as well. Check with some of your local charities, since some do recycle eyeglasses to the elderly and the poor. If you can't find such a charity, bite the bullet and toss all but the glasses you actually wear and one spare that sports a reasonably current prescription.

Files & Filing Cabinets
(see also Brochures, Desk, Mail, Office Supplies, Papers)

Organizing any filing system can be an awesome task, one most people put off as long as possible. Eventually, productivity grinds to a halt; the filing system conspires to sabotage nearly every working day. This holds true whether you are dealing with filing cabinets at your office or the household accounts and family records. You'll know it's time for drastic action when:
- You have no idea what happens to a document or piece of paper when you are finished with it;
- A piece of paper that you filed yesterday isn't there today, and you have no idea where it is;
- No one really understands the filing system;
- Papers in the files are older than you are;
- Someone spends some time nearly every day looking for mis-filed or lost papers and documents.

Next consider this:
- Eighty percent of everything that is filed is never going to be looked at again;
- Probably half of currently filed materials could be destroyed or moved to low-cost storage;

- •Nearly all of the records that are sent to storage are never looked at again;
- •There is no such thing as a functional, yet inexpensive filing cabinet (good ones are *always* expensive);
- •The typical four-drawer letter-sized filing cabinet requires seven to eight square feet of floor space (allowing for room to open the drawers), which costs dearly;
- •Add the cost of labor for maintaining the files (whether that labor comes from someone else or from yourself), along with the cost of supplies, and suddenly, filing a piece of paper adds up to a mighty expensive proposition!

Now that you've considered all of the above, consider this: just like death and taxes, paper is an unavoidable fact of life. If you, like so many others, are caught in a paper trap, it might be time to take charge and regain control of the paper in your life.

When you are ready to create or organize your home files, you'll need these basics:

> Filing cabinet(s)
> Hanging file folders (such as Pendaflex)
> Manila folders
> Labels for the tabs on the folders

When you buy filing cabinets, make sure that they are sturdy and have full-suspension, deep drawers. Full-suspension cabinet drawers open smoothly to the full extension, making it easy for you to see and deal with anything in the drawer. Bargain basement cabinets often have drawers that, if opened all the way, tip the cabinet dangerously and still don't provide a full view of everything in the drawer (items at the back of the drawer do not pull out into full view).

Hanging files are vital, whether you have one filing drawer or twenty, because they eliminate misfiling folders. The hanging file is *never* removed from the drawer. Instead, you pull out the manila folder (with the same label as that on the hanging file), and when you are ready to refile the manila folder, simply locate the hanging file with the corresponding label and drop the folder into it. You'll never misfile that folder behind another one again.

You'll want your cabinet to have rails to hold the hanging file folders, so if you already have a cabinet that doesn't have those, go to the stationery store and pick up an install-it-yourself metal rack to place inside the drawers. Unless absolutely necessary, don't get legal-sized cabinets. Everything about them is more expensive, especially the supplies, which you'll be buying well into the future. Legal cabinets are only worth the expense if the majority of your papers are legal sized. If you only have a few legal documents, they could be folded to fit into a less expensive, letter-sized cabinet.

Purging Current Files

To begin organizing your files, first purge any existing files. Go through each file individually:
- Keep financial records, but move records that are more than two years old into storage file boxes.
- Throw out all records that are outdated due to cost, such as travel and vacation or product price information.
- If you have an inordinate amount of memorabilia in the files (such as children's mimeographed schoolwork), select the best papers and throw the rest away.
- Get rid of expired policies and records pertaining to things you no longer own.
- Consider getting rid of at least 50 percent of all of the special pieces of paper that you had filed — like all of those interesting articles, amusing political cartoons, and outdated address lists.
- Get rid of all of the papers relating to previously completed charity work that has nothing to do with what's going on *now*.
- Weed out the correspondence files by keeping only what is active (such as letters dealing with disputes or ongoing issues like the upcoming family reunion). If you must save correspondence longer than two years, send those papers to storage.
- Never keep office supplies in the filing cabinet. Supplies belong in a supply cabinet or closet, not in the records and information storage area.

Setting Up New Files

As you purge your old files, you'll set up new ones. Use the KISS Rule (Keep It Simple, Stupid), and resist the urge to go hog-wild and establish dozens of categories. That just makes for more work and confusion later, so try to keep the number of categories down to an absolute minimum. Some examples of potential categories are:

•BUSINESS
•CLIENTS
•FINANCIAL
•GENERAL
•RESOURCES
•SPECIAL (Hobby or Special Interest)

Samples of possible files within those categories are:
FINANCIAL:
  Auto:
  Gasoline Bills
  Payments
  Repairs
  Registration
  Insurance:
  Auto (or under *Auto*)
  Health
  House
  Life
  Receipts:
  Credit Cards
  Department Stores
  Office Supplies
GENERAL:
  Articles
  Birth Certificate (copy)
  Career Information
  Children's Records
  Correspondence
  Medical Information (not bills)
  Pet Records
  Warranties & Instructions
BUSINESS (this is particularly useful if you have a small home-based business and need to keep these records separate from other household and/or hobby records):
  Correspondence
  Employee Records
  Expenses (business-related only)
  General Information
  Vendors (subtitled by name or product category)
CLIENTS (filed alphabetically by name)

Set up a filing system based on your particular needs and interests. As you clean up and implement your newly organized system, you can break it down even further (i.e., under *Articles,* you might want to list different *types* of articles). But however you decide to categorize, make up a hanging file and a manila file folder for each file. Make sure that the tab on the hanging file matches the wording on the manila file folder tab.

Leave the hanging folder in the drawer to permanently mark the proper placement of the file. Don't overstuff the folders. Too many papers start to choke up the file and obscure the information on the tab. To accommodate more papers in the file, crease along the lines scored at the bottom of the manila and hanging folder. This will provide a deeper bottom and allow for more papers in the file than would otherwise be possible. If you have done that and still have too many papers, simply hang another hanging folder behind the first file and add another file folder for that file, breaking it down chronologically, if you like. For example:

Correspondence   Jan-June 1989
Correspondence   July-Dec 1989

When you insert the plastic identification tags onto the hanging files, attach them to the *front* of the hanging folder, not the back. When your fingers touch that tab, the hanging file automatically opens up just a bit, giving you immediate access to the manila folder inside. If the tab is on the back side, your hand moves to the *next* file, which is not the one you want. And, although some studies show that it's more efficient to place all of the plastic tabs on one side — say the right side of the hanging file — I happen to be a proponent of staggered tabs. By staggering the plastic tabs on the hanging files — starting with the first position on the left, then inserting the next tab at the second position, and so on, until the whole drawer is staggered — you can open the drawer, and, without any digging, see at a glance the file you are searching for.

Set Limits

Set limits on your filing system. Begin with the actual cabinets. Never forget the cost of filing cabinets, the cost of the supplies that go into them, the time it takes to maintain the files, and the cost of square footage to house those paper-laden monsters. If you can set up your next system in one, or two, or three cabinets, do so, but vow not to exceed that number. You can do this by going through your files once or twice each year and weeding out papers that were filed unnecessarily or that have passed the two-year mark (move them to storage). Often you'll check a file and realize that you don't need *any* of the papers in that file. Toss the papers and reuse the file by applying a new label—thus saving supply expense. To limit the copying habit which can get totally out of hand ("put a copy of this in the Smith file and one in the Cooper file") try making "see also" notations on the front or inside cover of the file.

Limit yourself to one basic filing system, with the possible exception of *project files.* For people whose work generates large amounts of paper on a daily basis, project files can be helpful. These can be set up just as the permanent system is set up—with hanging folders and manila folders—and set into either the desk file drawer or into a rolling basket system that accommodates files. The basket can be used next to the desk on a daily basis, and when the project is over, the manila folders can be pulled out of the hanging folders and stored in transfile storage boxes. The hanging folders can be reused (you can buy extra blank tab inserts at the stationery store), and you can reorganize the cart or desk drawer with the appropriate folders for other project files.

Keeping the System Organized

Nobody likes to file—it's right up there with ironing and mowing the lawn in terms of satisfaction—but it needs to be done regularly in order to keep the system sensible and functioning. If you do it yourself, you can speed the process up a bit with the help of an alphabetical sorter (available at stationery stores). Try tackling the filing for ten minutes each day rather than waiting until it piles up to two hours' worth of tedium. And, as you put the papers in the folder, place the most recent paper in the front of the file, so that when you pull the file out the next time, the papers will be pretty much in chronological order.

If someone else does your filing, the challenge is to get them to file the papers in the same file that you might file them. This way, when that person is not available, you can theoretically walk over to the file and easily pull out exactly what you need. Since the person doing your filing is probably *not* a mind reader, it could be helpful if you would let him or her know what the piece of paper means to you in terms of filing category or topic. To do this, simply mark the paper with pencil, a highlighter pen, or a Post-it™ note. The person who files simply follows your instructions, and *voila!* the paper goes where it's supposed to, just waiting for the day when you need to call it back out of the files. Here's an example:

(Letter from) John Smith, Acme Corporation

- If you think of this person as Mr. Smith, highlight or mark *Smith.*
- If you think of this person as the connection to Acme Corporation, mark *Acme.*
- If this paper is not important enough for its own file, attach a Post-it™ and note (e.g.) *Customers, Miscellaneous.*

In the end, your filing system should work for you — not the other way around. Filing papers *into* the system — and, just as important, retrieving them — should be an uncomplicated function that you or those who work for you can perform without suffering a nervous breakdown.

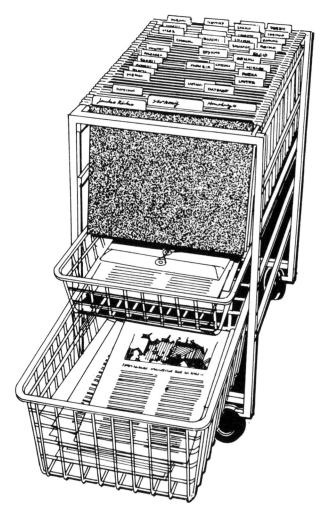

CLUTTER TRAPS

As I've said, you should limit yourself to one basic filing system. In spite of this fairly absolute principle, some people either want or feel they need additional filing methods to accommodate their papers. These methods include:

▼ **Accordion Files** — Don't use these if you value your sanity. It starts out fine, and goes downhill from there, as papers get mangled and mushed in the accordion folder. They get lost at the bottom of any one section of the accordion, and die without any help from you whatsoever. Occasionally an accordion folder can be called into temporary use as a transporter — to move lots of files from one location to another — but it should never be used as a filing system unto itself.

▼ **Tickler Files** — Tickler, or suspense, files have an up side and a down side. Generally, the divided categories in a tickler file include one through thirty-one (for the days of the month) and the months (January through December). When a piece of paper needs follow-up attention on a certain date (in the future) it is filed in the file folder for that date. If the follow-up is in a future month, it is filed in that month. Then, when that date rolls around, those papers requiring follow-up are checked and processed accordingly. On the first of each month, that month's file is checked, and its papers distributed among the one through thirty-one files for follow-up on specific dates of the current month.

With the hanging file and manila folder system, there is no reason that a tickler file couldn't help with successful follow-up for papers requiring dated attention. It is especially good for deadline-oriented projects and invoices that need to be paid by a certain date. A problem arises, however, when people start automatically storing papers in the tickler system without thinking about the *volume* of the paperwork that is accumulated in any one day's file. Hence, it's possible to pull the file on any given day and find, to your horror, that there is enough critical follow-up work in that day's folder alone to keep three people busy for two days straight. So, a tickler filing system can be a useful working tool, but only when used with extreme caution.

▼ **Pending Files** — These are the black holes of any filing system and are usually established so that action is taken, depending on when you get around to it. Unlike a specific tickler file, there is generally no date on a pending piece of paper. This is a general TO DO item, and therefore, should be placed in your TO DO basket to be *done*.

▼ **Indexing & Color Coding** — If you use the KISS Rule, why do you need an index? An index is just one more piece of work — you have to check it in order to locate a file, and you have to update it when files are added. I won't install them for clients because I've seen too many people who had them and still couldn't figure out their filing system or work efficiently with the system that the index represented.

Color coding is another trap. Color coding always seems like a nifty idea, but it almost never is. Once again, it's just more work. Before you decide what category a piece of paper gets filed under, you have to remember what *color* that category is in the first place. Then, you have to make sure you always have the right color-coded supplies on hand, or the paper can't be filed properly. It's a pain, and doesn't add anything except more work to the system. If you want to put your financial records in red folders and everything else in a neutral color, that's fairly logical. But when you have categories that include green for career, yellow for family and friends, red for financial, blue for resources, and so forth, you're setting yourself and your filing system up for certain self-destruction.

Furniture
(see also Antiques, Desk, Heirlooms)

Navigating through a room choked with furniture clutter can be daunting. There's your great grandma's Victorian settee, which is too uncomfortable to sit on, so it's piled with clutter. There's your desk from college — completely inappropriate as a work station for you now, so it also serves to store more clutter. Two more lamps than are needed to light the room, antique itty-bitty tables, and ornate cabinets occupy every inch of wall space, gathering dust on a daily basis. Mismatched bedroom sets, sofas, too many chairs, and folding card and game tables only add to the problem of furniture that takes up space and serves mainly to hold more clutter.

If furniture is cluttering up your space, you can give it away or sell it. If you are storing heirlooms in the basement or garage, shame on you. They'll get warped or water damaged, and then they won't be heirlooms, they'll be junk. This furniture should be used, given away, or sold. As you evaluate the furniture that you have, check for function. Credenzas, buffets, trunks, bookshelves, and end tables with drawers and cabinet space can do double duty—serving as furniture and storage space at the same time. Put a piece of glass over a wicker or antique trunk and you have a table that can also store any number of things, from blankets to games. If you're planning to replace or buy furniture, look for function. For the same amount of money, you can get a night stand next to the bed that has a drawer and a shelf rather than a night stand that has no storage capacity whatsoever. Old cabinets can be painted or stripped to provide storage for linens, records, sweaters, stationery supplies, and dishes. Don't let the stated purpose of any piece of furniture limit you. A buffet in the dining room doesn't have to hold china — it can store children's games or office supplies for your home-based business. A bookcase can hold baskets or bins with toys or craft supplies in them, and you can turn your bed into a piece of furniture that increases storage capabilities by adding underbed storage drawers. Even a coffee table can be functional. A table with a bottom shelf-like piece can hold magazines, knickknacks, newspapers, and the *TV Guide,* doubling the space of the table and eliminating clutter on the top of the table by providing space for storage underneath. The key word for all furniture is *functional.* If it's in the house (rather than the garage, basement, or attic), and it looks good and stores something at the same time, you've made your furniture aid and abet your organizational efforts—which should be a daily lifesaver in the fight to control clutter.

Gadgets
(see also Appliances, Hardware)

Gadgets could be called the epitome of clutter. According to Funk & Wagnall's *New Practical Standard Dictionary,* a gadget is "any small mechanical device or contrivance, especially one of which the name cannot be recalled." Gadgets are also those gizmos and doodads that everybody moves from place to place, muttering something about how "I know this belongs to something, I'm just not sure what . . . better keep it." For most people, these "small mechanical devices and contrivances" cover a plethora of items from appliances to jar openers. Gadgets are *supposed* to make life simpler, but somehow before that happens, the gadget becomes useless clutter.

Eventually gadgets find their way into drawers and cabinets in nearly every room of the house. The office is not exempt from this mechanical proliferation, either. Gadgets that probably go to the advanced telephone system or the new computer lounge on top of filing cabinets and inside desk drawers.

Where gadgets are concerned, fear rules the roost. Convinced that the gadget is a vital mechanical doodad that goes to a very important something or other, throwing the thing away becomes unthinkable. Being very low-tech myself, I can understand these fuzzy rationalizations for hoarding gadgets. I have them myself. But I do try to limit them. A box marked GADGETS sits on a shelf, with gadgets inside housed in plastic bags with a date, and, if I know what it goes to, that information as well. Once a gadget is dated past one year — particularly if I don't know what it is or what it goes to — it gets tossed. You can either save your unidentifiable archaic gadgets for a time capsule in the back yard, or date and destroy them as I do.

Games
(see also Children, Toys)

Games usually come in boxes, which we stack until the pile resembles a construction site. As soon as one game is pulled out from the stack, the stack collapses. Or the heavier boxes somehow move to the top by default, crushing all the boxes below. Obviously, games that are never played or games that have permanently missing pieces (making the game unplayable), should be either given away or tossed. Deniece Schofield, author of *Confessions of an Organized Housewife* and mother of five children, wrestled with the game problem and finally came up with what is probably the best solution to the care and storage of the rest of the games. Game boards and parts are removed from the box, the boards stacked on a shelf, and the parts stored in a metal parts cabinet (these cabinets have lots of different sized drawers). Deniece cuts the game directions from the lid of the box, photocopies them and puts the copies in a looseleaf notebook in alphabetical order. Directions that are on pamphlets are simply hole-punched and put into the binder. This method saves space and helps cut down on lost parts, directions, and mangled boxes. There are always some games that have parts that are too big for the cabinet — these few can be stored in the boxes as is.

If you have party games for adults (I don't mean X-rated here — we're talking, maybe, Trivial Pursuit), you can keep them away from sticky children's hands by storing them in a special place, such as a wicker trunk or the dining room buffet near the table where the games would actually be played. If you top the trunk with a piece of glass, it can be used as a game table as well. Keeping the family's games organized can only encourage playing together. After all, games are *fun,* not clutter!

Gardening Equipment & Supplies
(see also Catalogs, Tools)

Some people like yard and garden work and others hate it. Whether you love it or loathe it, yard work of any kind will be easier to face if the supplies and equipment are easy to store and retrieve.

You can begin by rounding up all of the gardening supplies, including those five pairs of old gloves, three rakes, pesticides and herbicides, fertilizers, sprayers, and so forth. Review the sprays, powders, and poisons and dispose of outdated materials. Keep these items in a secured cabinet so that children or pets can't get to them. Or you can store these supplies, along with small gardening tools, in a bench that doubles as a storage bin (secure the latch with a padlock). Long-handled tools can be hung on the wall from hooks or supported by two or three nails. If you're short on hanging space, group these tools in a large metal trash can. Small tools can be stored in bins by category, or, if you only use a few tools, they can be kept in a supply caddy or basket and carried to and from the garden as is. Don't forget overhead garage rafters for storage of major equipment and out-of-season lawn furniture. Dowels or brackets, mounted on the wall, can also hold big items such as wheelbarrows and furniture. Hoses can be stored on a reel with wheels or on a reel mounted next to the water spigot in a garden shed, basement, or garage. Planters and pots are best kept on shelves, with bags of potting soil stored in small covered buckets or trash cans. A work table near the potting materials can be a plus. Once the equipment is organized, there won't be any excuses not to do the work. And the next time the neighbor needs to borrow something, at least you'll know right where it is.

Gifts
(see also Cards, Souvenirs, Ties, Toys, Vases,
Wallets, Wine)

Gift clutter may be the most difficult clutter of all to deal with. After all, it was a *gift.* Never mind that it's the ugliest thing you've seen come down the pike in forty years—it was the *thought* that counted. So, now that you've *thought* about it, why not get rid of it by doing the logical thing—give it as a gift to someone else, or give it to charity. If the gift-giver visits you frequently and expects to see the gift displayed prominently, the problem is a bit stickier. Can you redecorate or gain a few pounds (or, better yet, lose a few pounds), making the gift obviously inappropriate for the new you? If the gift was lovingly handmade, recycling or tossing it is usually out of the question. You can use it and hope it breaks or disintegrates, or you can put it in a "treasure chest" where you can let everyone know you keep all of your treasures.

Getting rid of a gift often involves more guilt than is called for, so to spare yourself the gut-wrenching feelings that accompany dumping gifts that are duds, employ a little preventative maintenance. Let people know that you are not in the market for gifts, unless it's a gift of their time spent with you. They'll be secretly relieved at the financial savings, and you won't get your hopes up at your gift prospects only to have them dashed with yet another goofy present that you must act thrilled about receiving. If people insist on spending their hard-earned money on you, have them buy tickets to the movies, the theater, or the concert hall, and spend the evening with them at the event. You'll remember it longer than a gift you have to add to your inventory of conspicuous clutter.

Handbags

(see also Clothes, Cosmetics, Keys, Wallets)

Whenever I think of the clutter in handbags, I am reminded of the old Art Linkletter television show, "People Are Funny." Art used to go through women's handbags (with their permission). He would pick someone at random, and his TV viewers would watch as he looked on, supposedly stunned, at the contents of the woman's handbag. It was all very funny. Sometimes I think women today still think it's amusing to have a handbag full of just about everything but the kitchen sink. The fact is, the average onlooker does *not* think it is amusing to stand and wait while someone paws through her purse searching for her card, money, or keys. The average person finds this annoying and probably makes an unflattering judgment call right then about your competency—only because you've got a handbag bursting at the seams with clutter.

You can begin to correct this clutter problem (and at the same time clean up your image) by cleaning your handbag out and redistributing what you find there. The inventory in the average cluttered handbag can include:

Appointment book	Mirror
Address book	Note pad
Aspirin	Paperback book
Bills	Pens & pencils
Birth control devices	Other purses to organize
Business cards	things inside the handbag
Change purse	Receipts for purchases
Checkbook	Rolaids, mints, or gum
Cigarettes and lighter	Safety pins
Credit cards	Scraps of paper with ad-
Grocery list	dresses, phone numbers,
Hairpins & clips	or other miscellaneous
Hairbursh and/or comb	information
Handkerchief or tissues	Sewing repair kit
Keys	Sunglasses
Lotion	Tampons
Makeup	Wallet

A glance at that list explains why some people think women are stronger than men. Between bearing and caring for babies and hauling around a twenty-pound handbag every day, women have got to be either as strong as, or as stubborn as, a mule. A mugger would likely think twice before heisting one of these handbags — the weight of the thing would make a quick getaway on foot practically impossible.

A handbag need not serve as drugstore, stationery store, and portable office. A handbag should hold *essentials* only — money, a credit card or two (you don't need to carry all twenty-two of your cards), driver's license, checkbook, and perhaps a comb, lipstick, and blush for makeup. If you're carting around three lipsticks, four eyeshadows, cream base makeup, powders, and blushers by the numbers, it's time to get an overnight bag or a facelift. Aspirin, mint, gum, and candies all play havoc on your stomach and teeth, so cut back to the bare essentials (there's that word again). Discreet personal items should be carried if you're going to be away for the evening, but a minimum quantity should suffice — no need to lug around dozens of anything — from birth control pills to tampons. Your appointment and address book should be combined in one easy-to-use planner that you carry separately from your handbag, so that your handbag is home only to your cash and personal items. (If you carry a briefcase, you can either carry your appointment/address planner in your hand or in your briefcase.)

You can keep your receipts, business cards, grocery list, etc., all in this planner, leaving your handbag that much more clutter-free. If paperwork from your profession spills over into your daily life, get a briefcase and put it there, with your appointment book. Nothing is more disconcerting than to have a professional woman hold up a meeting while she searches for something in her bag. Keys can be kept at your fingertips by hooking them with a key clamp to the inside strap of your bag.

Paperback books also should be carried separately. If you start carrying things instead of stuffing them in your handbag, you'll reevaluate the need to haul it around in the first place.

Finally, to cure yourself of the cluttered handbag syndrome, get small handbags. Big handbags invite clutter; smaller bags demand discipline. Smaller handbags can also be worn bandolier-style, which means that purse snatchers are more likely to pass you by, and it reduces the chances of setting your handbag down and forgetting to pick it up again as you walk out the door.

Hardware

(see also Gadgets, Electrical Supplies,
Junk Drawer, Tools)

Hardware can cover everything from gadgets to screws to tools. For our purposes, hardware means nuts, bolts, screws, picture hangers, wire, and all of the other small assorted handy-Dan stuff that lands either in a box somewhere or in the dumping ground of last resort — the junk drawer.

If it doesn't land in the junk drawer (usually because the junk drawer is already full to bursting), the hardware starts mating indiscriminately in coffee cans, cigar boxes, shoe boxes and on work tables. Tools, gadgets, electrical supplies, glue, pieces of wood and metal, nails of every description, and assorted other pieces of unnamed hardware commingle, until eventually it turns into one big mess that means at least fifteen minutes of digging before the required doodad is located and retrieved.

Whatever method you use to store these items, weed out those odd pieces that have been lying around for years, waiting to be used for "something." If it has rusted, if you can't imagine what it goes with or could ever possibly be used for, get rid of it. Useless pieces of hardware, contribute to a clutter problem that even the handiest Dan or Danielle could well live without.

Hats

(see also Closets, Clothes, Collections)

Depending on your fashion sense, personality, and the climate, you're likely to have any number of hats. There are winter hats, ski caps, Easter bonnets, baseball caps, boating hats, tennis visors, rain hats, and funny hats — like that hysterical cap with the huge antlers on it that you got from the gang on your thirtieth birthday. Multiply these hat possibilities by the number of people in your family, and the potential for headgear clutter is virtually unlimited.

First, go through all of your hats and eliminate anything that is damaged, stretched, or so stupid that you never wear it. If you have trouble getting rid of some of those hats — like that cap with the antlers on it, or the humongous sombrero that you carted back from Mexico — try reminding yourself that you are an adult, and unless you plan to wear it on Halloween, get rid of it. Ditto old turbans,

---

☑️ CLUTTER CHECKLIST

Here are some suggestions for organizing and storing it all so that when you need a particular screw you can lay your hands on it without examining every screw in the house (see also Storage: Clutter Containers section):

❑ **Metal Parts Cabinet** — These cabinets have plastic drawers that are sized to hold screws, nails, nuts and bolts, and the like. Assuming you have the patience to put the nails or screws into the proper drawer when you put them away (as opposed to tossing them into a box or drawer), these can keep your inventory nicely organized.

❑ **Glass Jars** — Glass jars of all sorts can be used to store hardware by size, and provide an instant view of what lies within the container. Baby food jars or sample jelly jars are small enough to perfectly store those tiny pieces of hardware that might otherwise get lost in the shuffle. To cut down on the space these jars occupy, install a shelf in your garage or basement and put some of the jars on the shelf. Attach the lids of the remaining jars to the *underside* of the shelf with a lock washer so that it stays fixed to the shelf. When you need something in one of those jars, unscrew the *jar* instead of the lid, and replace it in the same manner.

outdated Easter bonnets, and sports caps that have seen better days. A word about hat collections: If you can't bear to part with it, a collection should be displayed, so get those hats up on the wall or get rid of them. If they are so funny and/or fabulous, you should let everybody you know see them.

Heirlooms

(see also Antiques, Dishes, Furniture, Jewelry, Linens, Photographs)

"I inherited this, what could I do?" is a wail that I've heard time and time again from clutterbugs. If you're like a lot of people, you pack it, stack it, and do everything but use it. Stuffed in basements, garages, and attics, and hidden in trunks and the far reaches of closets, heirlooms go unused and unappreciated. Inherited treasures cover the gamut from Grandpappy's golf trophies to furniture that you wouldn't be caught dead sitting on. Throw in that

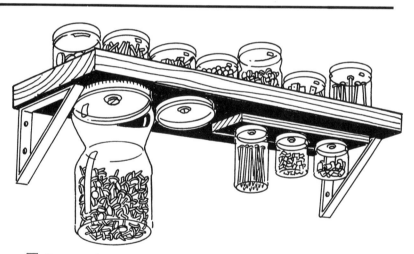

❑ **Drawer Dividers** — If a drawer is your choice for storage, try to keep some order with cutlery dividers. Small sample jelly jars also fit into drawers, and you can even put cigar boxes (without the lids) into drawers to serve as containers for certain categories of items.

❑ **Boxes** — Boxes, including cigar boxes, gift-type boxes, coffee cans, and tea tins can be used to hold hardware and can be stacked on a shelf. Be sure you mark the outside of the boxes on all sides — *screws, wire, large nails,* etc. — so you don't have to check every box to get to the one you need for any given project.

☑ CLUTTER CHECKLIST

You can organize the hats you wear on a fairly regular basis in several different ways:

❏ **Drawers** — If you've got any drawer space, knit hats and caps can be stored flat inside.

❏ **Boxes** — A Lucite sweater box serves as good storage for out-of-season hats and caps. Put it under the bed or on a shelf.

❏ **Baskets** — Winter caps and hats — especially the children's — can be stored in a basket by the door. Establishing the habit of dropping hats in the basket as soon as they're taken off should mean fewer missing hats and no more frantic searches for hats on the way out the door.

❏ **Pegs** — Hooks and pegs that you can install yourself also do a good job of holding hats. One simple peg system is an expanding wooden mug rack that can be installed on the back of the door or in the entry area.

❏ **Coat Trees** — These oldies but goodies are terrific in a corner of the entry and can hold coats and hats right where they are most needed — by the door.

❏ **Wig Forms** — Wig forms can be nailed to a closet shelf and dressy hats can be placed on the head, insuring that the hat keeps its shape and doesn't get smushed.

❏ **Hat Boxes** — Hat boxes are back and are available through catalogs and organizational retail outlets. They can hold just about anything, but are especially good for holding, would you believe it, *hats*.

---

silver service for twelve (that you never use because you never entertain) and that wooden butter churn (when did you last churn butter?) and suddenly all those heirlooms reveal their true purpose: clutter.

Perhaps you're afraid if you use it you'll damage it. Yet, many antique items were crafted by hand and are sturdier than anything we could possibly find today. If your heirloom is too delicate to be functional, use it to display something else. A delicate piece of furniture can hold plants or family photographs rather than serve as a table for daily meals or as a chair to sit on. Antique clothing can be remade into jackets, blouses, or christening gowns for the babies born *today*. Jewelers can often repair antique jewelry; antique letters and photographs should be preserved in an acid-free environment and stored appropriately or put into family albums. If you aren't interested in any of these ideas, why not pass the heirlooms along to your family today? Somebody near and dear to you doesn't have a set of silver, so this holiday season why not pass Grandma's monogrammed silver along to them so they can use it for their special occasions? Heirlooms should be passed to family members with love, not stored out of sight, to be forgotten until someone (you) passes on.

HOARD A storage place, especially of treasure; a hidden reserve; that which has been accumulated. Or, what you do on a daily basis to keep your collection of clutter intact and growing.

Holiday Decorations
(see also Boxes, Candles, Packing Materials)

Holiday decorations, including wrapping paper, ribbons, ornaments, and other special items—from mangers to Halloween skeletons—tend to get stuffed into a box, drawer, or closet. When they reemerge they are squashed or broken, necessitating a last-minute trip to the store to replace them.

Other decorations accumulate, year by year, until you find yourself with five times more than you'll ever use. Yard figures that you never put out anymore, ten more strings of lights than you have time to put up, Easter baskets and bunnies that you keep even though the kids are grown, angel hair, fake snow, and Thanksgiving turkey cutouts all grow into a mountain of decorations that you can't bear to deal with when the holiday comes around. Face the holiday facts. Weed out the stuff that you never use and organize what's left, so that decorating at holiday time can be an event to look forward to, rather than an event you dread.

Proper storage can cut down on repeat purchases, and can make getting the decorations down and putting them back an easier task to face. The Clutter Checklist offers some storage ideas, but however and wherever you store your decorations, be sure to clearly mark all sides of the boxes by holiday, and keep them all in one place, if possible. By doing this, you can help reduce the digging that occurs before every holiday, along with the aggravation that goes along with what is supposed to be a pleasant event.

Husbands

Putting one's spouse in the same category as clutter can be a bit misleading. After all, strictly speaking, he's not the clutter exactly; but in a lot of cases, he is the originator and/or creator of vast quantities of clutter that eventually cannot be overlooked or even tolerated. Since tossing one's husband (or live-in mate, boyfriend, or roommate—you know—the other half) out with other clutter is generally not a viable solution, the question becomes more focused: "How can I make him clean up his clutter and get organized?" Answer: You probably can't *make* that person do anything about

---

☑ CLUTTER CHECKLIST

❏ **Boxes**—People tend to save gift boxes thinking they'll recycle them at a holiday. What inevitably happens, however, is that only a few get reused and the rest get pushed and shoved around in the closet. Save a half-dozen boxes if you must, but make sure that they all fit into one another to cut down on the storage space they require. Beyond that, it is far cheaper to buy gift boxes as the holiday approaches than it is to allocate expensive square footage for storing them.

❏ **Paper**— The amount of paper kept on hand could be reduced substantially if people wouldn't buy only Christmas paper for Christmas and only birthday paper for birthdays, and so on. Check out the large selection of all-occasion wrapping paper that has no message printed on it. Glossy white paper with a pretty ribbon will do at Christmas, for a wedding, and a birthday; a red-striped paper will cover all of those and Valentine's Day as well. By having neutral paper, you won't have to store Christmas or birthday paper until the event rolls around again. But since you can actually use all-occasion wrapping paper *throughout* the year, store it so it's accessible. You can put it in the closet in a gift wrap organizer, (made of heavy cardboard and available at variety stores or through catalogs), or you can stand rolls up in a small round wastebasket. Flat paper can be stored in a plastic sweater box and put on a shelf, or if you have drawer space, that can serve as storage as well. Keep an extra pair of scissors and tape with the paper so you don't have to search high and low for them every time you need to wrap something.

---

his mess, particularly once it has reached an advanced state. People get organized when they are good and ready, and not a moment before. You may think it's a problem, but if he doesn't think it's a problem, the situation won't change. He's happy with the clutter, and is convinced that you are the one with the problem. In this case, just about the only possible solution to this common domestic scenario is the Yours, Mine, and Ours Rule.

This philosophy holds that, contrary to traditional beliefs, it is not really all *ours*. There's *yours*. There's *mine*. And there's *ours*. And, if you're smart, you'll set it up that way, and keep it that way. It can save you trips to the therapist's office and/or the divorce court.

❏ **Miscellaneous Decorations** — Other decorations, such as streamers, scenes, paper skeletons, and wreaths need to be stored in a box and labeled clearly, by holiday, if possible. You can store boxes under the bed, or, if you must, in the garage or attic — but only if those areas are clean. Make sure the decorations are put back into the box neatly. If they are thrown into the box and put away, when they are pulled out again they will probably be a useless mess. Special candles can be stored near the dining room or kitchen in a covered basket or on a higher shelf. These candles might be usable for other special occasions, if you think about it, so the closer they are kept to the table, the better.

❏ **Ornaments** — Although you can pack your ornaments with newspaper in a carton, most of the time this means at least one or more broken ornaments. Why? Mainly because these delicate items need special packing, and regardless of how carefully they are packed, it's usually not good enough and something gets squished. It is much better to pack the ornaments into ornament boxes, which offer extra protection because there is a compartment for each ornament. (You can buy these at variety stores or through catalogs.) Next year you'll be less likely to be unpleasantly surprised with a broken ornament when you open the box.

❏ **Lights** — Untangle the lights *before* they are packed by looping them around a piece of cardboard. Consider replacing any burned out lights now, since after the holiday they'll probably be on sale. When it's time to put them up again you will have saved yourself a trip to the store.

Here's how it works: He wants to make and live in a mess, fine. That's *his* mess. He can have it. Map out an area—a room, the garage, the dining alcove—and call it his. If you can shut the door on it, all the better. If you can't—say it's a corner in a too-small apartment—learn to wear blinders when you pass by that area. Remember, it's his. Then, there's *yours.* Pristine and perfectly perfect. Yours. As in, keep your disorganized self away from this part of the house. It's mine. Then there's *ours.* This is where you actually commingle and compromise. The other person will have to tidy up a bit; you'll have to loosen up your standards a bit. Compromise in the name of the relationship. You don't have to sacrifice all of your organized ethics, but you'll probably have to let go of some of them. And the other person in your life will have to incorporate a little shaping up into this (dis)orderly routine. Thus you come to that all-loving state known as *ours.*

Sooner or later every relationship, in my opinion, hits a crisis point over how things are kept up around the place. I believe that those couples who opt for the Yours, Mine, and Ours method of environmental matrimony pass through the crisis with not only more wisdom and love in their hearts, but a sense that each person has actually *won* the battle to have it their way. Since each of you thinks you have won, each of you will head into the next twenty years with a satisfied, albeit smug, little smirk on your face and in your heart.

IN•VEN•TO•RY The supply of stock or materials on hand, which in your case is *substantial.*

Invitations
(see Announcements)

Jewelry
(see also Clothes, Heirlooms)

Jewelry, like everything else, needs to be sorted with an eye to possible elimination of some pieces. Begin your culling process by getting rid of that fuzzy frog pin with the "jeweled" eyes, those day-glow earrings from your hippie days, that charm bracelet from high school, and that twenty-dollar watch that has been broken for years.

Gift pieces of jewelry that you've never worn, and likely never will wear, should be given away. Broken costume jewelry should either be repaired pronto or given to children for dress-up (so long as it is in safe condition), donated to a charity, or thrown in the trash. Jewelry that's tangled should be sorted out (work on it while you're watching television), and jewelry that needs to be cleaned should be cleaned—either by you or the jeweler.

Jewelry boxes can be serviceable for jewelry, *if* you don't have a large inventory. The boxes are really not made to hold *lots* of jewelry and they end up looking pretty on the outside and hiding a jumbled mess on the inside. A variation of this idea is to place divided organizers into a drawer, and put all of your jewelry in the compartments. There are organizers made especially for this purpose, and they are covered in moiré taffeta, making your drawer attractive as well as functional.

Silver jewelry can be stored in special storage pouches treated to keep the jewelry tarnish-free. You can attach a gift tag to the bag

---

☑ CLUTTER CHECKLIST

When you've given your jewels the once over, you can reorganize them with some simple gadgets and ideas:

❑ **Earrings**—Earrings can be hooked onto an earring holder (usually found in clear plastic with slots to hold pierced earrings). You can also place a piece of foam in a drawer, and stick post earrings into the foam, keeping the backs in a small separate box.

❑ **Necklaces**—Necklaces can be kept in good order by hanging them on hooks or on a chain keeper (generally a chain keeper is made of clear plastic, holds several necklaces, and sits on top of a counter or dresser). You can even hang a mug rack in your closet or in the dressing area to hang your necklaces on—tangle free and in clear view for easier selection when you dress.

❑ **Pins**—Pins can be kept in their own small box, or stuck into a pretty, small satin pillow that you can keep inside a drawer or on your dressing table.

❑ **Rings**—Rings are easily lost, and usually have sentimental value, so giving them their own special resting place in a small ring box (these will hold several rings) or drawer can be a good idea. If you take off rings when you shower or wash dishes, have a hook or covered box next to the sink so that you automatically put the rings there when you take them off. You'll reduce the risk of lost, drowned rings substantially.

with the piece of jewelry listed on it so you don't have to look through each bag to find what you want when you need it. And of course, valuable gems that are worn only once in a great while should be stored in a safe or safety deposit box. But in the end, unless you are keeping those gems for investment purposes, if you aren't wearing them, why are you storing them? Maybe now is the time to sell them, and either invest the money, or buy something else. If you're saving that good jewelry to pass on to your heirs, consider passing it on now. They'll enjoy wearing it, and you'll enjoy seeing them wear it. Remember, just because something is valuable, doesn't mean it isn't clutter.

JUNK Pieces of old cable or rope used especially to make mats, gaskets, mops, or oakum; old metal, glass, paper, or other trash that may be reused in some form; secondhand, worn or scrapped articles of trivial value; a shoddy product; something insignificant. Or, all of the above, which, as fate would have it, now shares your living and working quarters with you.

Junk

Junk is a relative term. One person's junk is another's treasure, so it really depends on who is looking at the item(s) in question.

What's Your Definition of Junk?

Mark everything that you think is *junk*. Then give the list to someone else close to you and see if they agree.
- __ Antique dental equipment
- __ College essays and notes
- __ Baby clothes (your kids are grown)
- __ Broken radio from 1954
- __ High school letter sweater (moth-eaten)
- __ Collection of 500 copies of *National Geographic*
- __ Rock collection
- __ Sticker collection
- __ Bobbing plastic hula girl from Hawaii
- __ Size 8 evening gowns (you are a size 14)
- __ Tin box full of keys
- __ Ripped jeans

__ Stationery printed with outdated address
__ Old telephone
__ Dried-up paint
__ Wooden paddle from your fraternity
__ Broken VCR
__ Ping pong table with three legs

If you are convinced that your clutter is *not* junk, then your options are to use it, lose it, or store it (a limited option at best). If you have reached the conclusion that you own pure, unadulterated junk, then give it away (but only to someone who doesn't think it is junk — it isn't nice to make charities haul your junk away when you know they won't be able to make dignified use of the items). While you are defining what is and isn't junk, consider how annoyed you become when other people refer to your stuff as junk. *You* do what you have to do with your things, but never lose sight of the junk issue. And the next time you hear yourself starting to call someone else's stuff *junk,* bite your hypocritical tongue.

Junk Drawer
(see also Batteries, Electrical Supplies, Gadgets)

Everybody has at least one junk drawer, including me. Even though most junk drawers are an organizational horror, I happen to think this type of drawer is good for the soul. Nobody's perfect, after all, and the junk drawer is proof positive of this. It is effort enough to clean it out when you are gabbing on the phone. If it's not near the phone, clean it out when it won't shut any more.

I'm never surprised at what I find in junk drawers (and that includes my own) and neither should you be. You're likely to come across screws, wire, rubber bands, extension cords, decks of cards, seed packets, matchbooks, glue, unidentified keys, a knob from something you can't identify . . . you know the scene.

The best way to clean out a junk drawer is to throw away at least 25 percent of what is in there. After that, you can try drawer dividers, but junk drawers being what they are, that probably won't help for long (though it helps somewhat). You can divide things into cigar boxes (inside the drawer) or, if the drawer is deep enough, shoe boxes. If there's anything there that goes somewhere else — like a toy, for instance — put it in the room where it belongs. Other than that, there's not much hope for the junk drawer, so I wouldn't worry about it too much. When one junk drawer turns into two or three, *then* you can worry.

Keys

(see also Handbags)

Invariably, when people attack the clutter problem, keys crop up all over the place. The tendency is to keep those loose keys, even though *nobody knows what they unlock.* They must be to *something,* is the rationale, and chances are, that's true. But that something could be anything from the last house you lived in, to old locks that have since been replaced, to a defunct bicycle lock, to your college boyfriend's apartment. Given the possibilities, both past and present, you should examine the keys and try to figure out what in the house, office, or car they might unlock. Try them out (this does help solve the mystery, you know), and if the key goes to something, identify it with a tag and put it in a key box or cabinet. If you can't find out what the key goes to, *throw it away.* An exception to this might be any keys that look like they might open a safety deposit box. Safety deposit box keys are always disappearing, so when you find a likely candidate for somebody's safety deposit box, put it by the door, and the next time you go to the bank, check it out, or check with your relatives to see if they know of a safety deposit possibility that you may have overlooked or forgotten.

Keys that you carry with you can also outgrow their original purpose. People who own a business can find themselves bogged down with house, office, and warehouse keys, resulting in a weighty key ring that is virtually undecipherable—nobody really knows what goes to what except the holder of the magic ring. People sometimes feel that owning and using twenty keys per day makes them awfully important, and you can hear that importance clanking well in advance of the Important Person's actual arrival. It is possible that not everyone agrees with the key-induced VIP assessment, but if you must wear your importance on a key ring, at least mark each key so that, should anyone else have to handle all of those important opening and closing duties, they will know what fits what. While you are marking keys, force yourself to give up those that don't go to anything anymore. I'm sure you'll still clank enough to feel secure in your own importance.

If you've got a clutter problem in your home or office, chances are good that you are losing your keys among the debris with alarming regularity, resulting in last-minute delays as you look for your keys. To put a stop to these frantic searches, establish a key drop near the door of your home or office. A basket or a hook next to the door can serve as the place to drop keys the instant you come in, and they will be waiting for you to grab on your way out again.

To end time-consuming digging through an oversized and overstuffed handbag to find your keys when you are out and about, attach them to a key hook-style clamp, and hook them to your handbag strap. You'll save yourself a search at your car or house door, and, more important, it will discourage would-be muggers (and worse) who tend to look for people who are fumbling or otherwise distracted as they enter their house or car.

Kitchen Utensils
(see also Appliances, Dishes, Pots & Pans)

Kitchen utensils multiply mercilessly until there are drawers full of spatulas, can openers, wooden spoons, wire whisks, spaghetti twirlers (huh?), pastry blenders, egg beaters, corn on the cob holders, meat thermometers and dozens of whatchamacallits and assorted thingamajigs. To make matters worse, duplicates pop up all over the place—*two* potato mashers, *three* cheese graters, *four* identical garlic presses (you bought one when you thought you misplaced the first one, and the other two were gifts), and unidentifiable doodads too numerous to count. Appliance parts that you suspect (but don't know for certain) belong to the blender, food processor, mixer, and/or pressure cooker, complete the mess.

To counteract this proliferation, first get rid of unnecessary duplicates and utensils that, let's face it, you *never* use. Rarely used gourmet gadgets that stand as mute testament to your culinary abilities can go as well. Miscellaneous attachments and parts should be examined and matched up with the correct appliances. Put these parts in a drawer by themselves, or store them in a labeled box in the cabinet so you don't have to reach past them to get to the spatula for the serious business of flipping pancakes and eggs. Silly gift items can go as well. That set of porcelain Japanese soup spoons can hit the giveaway decks, since you have never used the things and probably won't. Go through your flatware and clear out anything that does not actively contribute to the business of daily cooking and eating. Unless you have dozens of family members chowing down at your place every day, three sets of flatware is, at best, redundant.

After you have weeded out the excess, you can store your utensils either in drawers, containers, or on wall-mounted racks; just remember to keep items as close to their functional area as possible. Flatware should be by the dishes so that setting the table is an organized event. Keep knives near the cutting board and cooking utensils near the stove.

Utensils stored in drawers can be organized using cutlery trays, or by making your own dividers with boxes and divided trays that are available at variety organizing stores and through catalogs. Knives can be stored (with caution, especially if you have children) in a knife block or on a wall-mounted magnetic strip knife rack. Often-used wooden spoons and the like can be stored upright in a ceramic jar near the stove or work area. Many utensils such as spatulas and large turning forks have a hole in the handle so they can be stored on hooks or pegs on the wall near the stove — also a good idea. Some people refuse to hang utensils for fear they'll get dirty, but if you are only keeping things you use regularly, these items will be washed so often that there won't be any dirt buildup.

Once you've cleared out the clutter and creatively organized and stored the remaining utensils, remember that in the future, unless you are the world's most accomplished cook, you won't need to increase your utensil inventory beyond the basics that you already have on hand. After all, Grandma was a great cook and she didn't have all of those gadgets, so why should you?

Knickknacks

(see also Collections, Memorabilia, Salt & Pepper Sets, Souvenirs)

The thing to remember about knickknacks is that accumulating them usually starts off innocently. You pick one up as a souvenir, or you pick up, say, a cat figurine, because you have a soft spot for cats. Before you know it, you have souvenir spoons from the four corners of the globe and that first cat figurine has multiplied a hundredfold, growing with every birthday and holiday. The bottom line on knickknacks is that they take up space and require endless dusting and cleaning; in California, they're the first to go in an earthquake. If your collection is carefully packed, on the other hand, you don't have to dust them and they might survive a quake. But what good are they in a box?

Keeping a knickknack collection from turning into clutter can be as simple as assigning one cabinet for knickknacks, and no more. Encourage friends and relatives *not* to give you knickknacks by telling them that your collection is complete and you're not interested in adding to it. That takes care of future knickknack clutter. For current knickknack clutter, consider going through the knickknacks and selecting a few to pass on to friends and relatives. You can also give some to charity or to a few people in a nursing home to brighten up their rooms. Remember, each knickknack you unload saves you space and the time it takes to keep it clean and dusted. Over a year, that time saved probably adds up to at least enough time to go out and kick up your heels now and then. You won't need a special occasion to do it — you can just call a knickknack holiday. It sure beats dusting.

Lamps

Extra lamps are always hidden in some closet or attic corner, waiting to be fixed. It's a good lamp, after all, and it only needs the doohickey replaced or a glue repair job or a new shade, and it'll be fine. Or, it's part of a pair (nobody knows this but you) and as soon as the other is fixed, we'll use it — can't break up a pair after all (uh, how long has this pair been broken up so far?). These lamps have probably been waiting for their minor surgery and/or new shade for months, even years, but there they sit, lighting up absolutely nobody's life. Rather than waiting for a member of the family to tackle this do-it-yourself fix-it project, gather up all of these lamps, take them to a repair shop, and get them fixed. Now comes the acid test; when you bring them back, where are you going to put them? It seems to me that if you've been blessed with enough light all this time without needing the light of these broken lamps, then you probably don't need more. Furthermore, you might not have a spare dresser, table, or spot on the floor to put the things anyway. If this sounds like you, save your money and your time, and just give the lamps to charity to fix and distribute.

Laundry
(see also Bathroom Clutter, Closets,
Clothes, Linens)

When clutter starts to get out of control, there's almost always some laundry making a contribution to the mess. Both clean and dirty laundry tends to pile up in baskets, laundry bags, and on the floor and chairs. Before you know it, you're digging through the dryer to find some clean underwear because someone threw dirty clothes in with the last basket of clean, not-yet-folded clothes. Not only that, but the clothes that were earmarked for charity somehow got mixed in with the dirty clothes, and now you can't remember what was giveaway and what was keep. You wind up resorting clothes and digging through piles on an almost daily basis.

To regain control of the laundry, first go through the house and gather up *all* of the clothing that's piled up and stuffed into baskets, boxes, or bags. Put it all in one area and SORT. Have a box for CHARITY, one for WASH, one for DRY CLEANING, one for

REPAIR, and one for CLEAN and/or IRON. Enlist some help. Have your helper fold the clean clothes as you find them, setting the ironing aside. Next throw in a load of wash, and while that's running, check the repair pile and start mending. If the repair pile is huge, you can do one of two things; take it to a person who repairs clothes for money (highly recommended) or commit to repairing two items per evening before bed. Put the dry cleaning in the car, or get someone (a teenager is good here) to take those clothes to the cleaners, *now.* On the way to the cleaners, drop off the charity items. Don't wait for the charity to come to you, because by the time they get there, you and other members of the family will have gone through the CHARITY box and pulled stuff back out, wailing about the heartlessness of trying to give that beloved old sweatshirt away.

If your wash amounts to five loads or more, go to a laundromat, even if you do have your own washer and dryer. At the laundromat you can do *ten* loads of wash at a time if you want, and not be distracted to the point where you leave a load in the dryer for three days and forget to get on with the other nine loads of wash. Fold the clothes *before* you put them in the basket, and they'll be ready to go directly into drawers and closets.

Cleaning Up Your Act

Once the backed-up laundry clutter is organized, a little future planning is in order. Ongoing laundry clutter control and organization starts with *responsibility.* Each person in the family can assume some of the responsibility for the clothes that go onto their bodies. Spouses and children over the age of five can all pitch in. They can start by (gasp!) picking up after themselves. No more dropping clothes on the floor, beds, and chairs. Pick them up, put them away, or drop them in laundry baskets. Have a dirty clothes hamper in each bedroom as well as in the bathrooms, and provide another hamper or two (at least one in the master bedroom) for dry cleaning—husbands, take note. You can put a REPAIR basket in the laundry room for things that need to be repaired, and you can also install a rod or get a portable clothes rack so that you can hang clothes as soon as they come out of the dryer, resulting in less ironing for you. (If you live in an apartment, you can stash your REPAIR basket in a closet or hang a canvas bag from a hook.)

Other things to keep in the laundry room are a basket to empty pockets into (saving your machines from coins, gum, and scraps of paper with important information), and another DRY

CLEANING basket for clothes inadvertently put into the "to be washed" pile. You can retrieve these later, when you are ready to go to the dry cleaners. (Apartment dwellers can keep this basket for change, etc., anywhere that is handy and near where the clothes are gathered and/or sorted.)

If you've got a family, do a load of wash each day. (To save time, have each family member take their laundry to the laundry room each morning.) Throw it in when you get up. By the time you have showered and roused everyone from their beds, the load will be ready for the dryer. By the time everybody gets through breakfast, that load will be dry and ready to fold. Now make someone in the family (not you) fold the stuff. If kids on farms can milk cows before they go to school, then other kids on this earth can fold a few clothes before they tear out of the house.

Apartment dwellers with no washer/dryer facilities need to be even more organized with their laundry. Plan to do it once each week, preferably on the same day. Real shortcuts include paying someone to do it for you, or sending sheets to the laundry, along with shirts and some pants. These can be dropped off as they accumulate (drop them off on the way to work, and pick them up on the way home) and will substantially cut down on the other washables that will have to be done at the commercial laundromat.

Even if you have your own washer and dryer, consider taking some of your clothes to a professional laundry. It doesn't cost as much as you might think and shirts, in particular, get great treatment at the professional laundry. The time you save by not having to do them yourself is irreplaceable. The same goes for some pants that need to be pressed and creased. Saturday is much more glorious when spent with friends or family instead of with the iron, ironing board, and a pile of laundry.

MUD•DLE To make turbid; to confuse or be confused; to mix up; make a mess of. Or, what you are in the middle of right now.

Linens
(see also Heirlooms, Laundry)

Linens, including towels, tablecloths, sheets, and the doilies made by your great-grandma, always seem like a necessity of daily life —

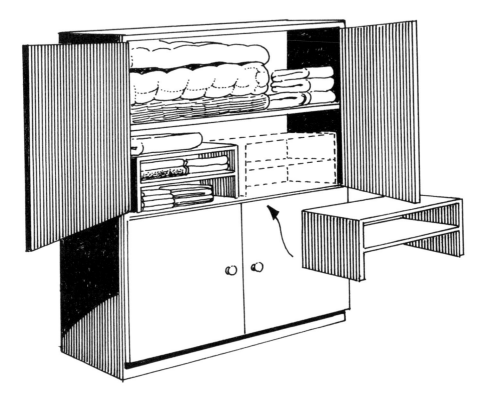

and some of them are. Obviously towels and washcloths are put to good use every day, and bedding is also a daily linen requirement. But tablecloths, doilies, and linen napkins tend to be stored for special occasions, and in some cases those items are actually never used at all. Perhaps you inherited the pieces and don't know what to do with them, so you store them with the other linens. Or maybe your tablecloths are round, and you don't have a round table any more, but it seems a shame to get rid of such expensive stuff now. Ultimately, the linens, good, bad, and daily, get piled into the linen cabinet to be pushed and shoved about as you struggle to get what you really need at any moment in time. The piles start to resemble towers, and invariably the stacks of linens collapse into each other, leaving you to handle your mounting frustration as you try to locate a *complete* set of sheets for the kid's bed, or a clean towel for your dripping body. To shorten the towers a bit, go through the linens and get rid of anything that can no longer be put to good use (such as the outdated tablecloths). Inherited items that you never use can be passed along to your heirs *now* so that they can make use of them in their homes. Raggedy sheets and towels that you really don't use can be turned into rags or tossed.

Once you've eliminated some of those linens, make more functional use of the remaining space by putting the special-occasion tablecloths and napkins in a special drawer, or, if you have no drawer, in a plastic sweater box. This will keep them neatly pressed and out of the daily inventory of linens that are constantly being shifted around. Store this box in the linen cabinet, in the buffet with your good dishes and silver, or, if you have exceptionally limited space, put it on a shelf in the pantry or in a closet. Everyday place mats and kitchen towels can be kept on instant add-a-shelves. A supply of fresh towels can be kept on a shelf mounted in the bathroom, so it's easy for anyone to grab a towel when they need it; this will also free up more linen cabinet space for bedding. Out-of-season blankets and the like can be stored in a wicker trunk or blanket box (the trunk can double as a bedside stand or table). You can install extra shelves in your linen cabinet, making each stack of linens smaller so that the sheets and pillowcases don't end up collapsing in a pile. If you've got different sized beds, mark the shelves with a label or a piece of tape — i.e., Twin, Queen — and when you put your sheets away, put them on the proper shelf. When bed-making time rolls around, whoever makes the bed can tell immediately which sheets to grab. If you are really short on linen storage space, consider storing the sheets on a closet shelf or in an underbed storage drawer in the bedroom where they're used. While you're at it, cut down on your housework obligations by making whoever sleeps in that bedroom responsible for changing their own bed and folding their own bed linens when they come out of the dryer. You'll be doing them a terrific favor. After all, folding linens and changing beds builds character, now doesn't it?

Love Letters
(see also Memorabilia, Papers)

Most people think love letters should be tossed as soon as you enter into a marriage or long-term live-in relationship. Not me. I think old love letters serve a very important purpose; they make you feel young and special, and can quite often serve as a quick pick-me-up on an otherwise dreadful day. Although I do think they can be thinned out as the years wear on, a selection of the very best deserve to go down in history with you. Besides weeding them out (volumes of letters can be egotistically excessive, after all), the important thing to do is to find an appropriate hiding place for the few you decide to keep around. It wouldn't do to have one's spouse or children poring over these tomes, so for now, tuck them away in some clever hiding place. When you are older, and presumably wiser, you can dig the letters out again. Grandchildren will be delighted to read them, and in the name of family history you (devil, you) will, of course pass them along. By then, the letters will be considered thrilling, and serve as a testament to your long and terribly exciting life.

Lumber

Scrap lumber lurks wherever there is a do-it-yourselfer or a tinkerer. "Don't throw that out," grunts the do-it-yourselfer, "that's perfectly good wood." Good for *what,* I'd like to know, and more importantly, *when* is this perfectly good wood going to be put to use? The stuff piles up in all sizes and shapes, virtually impossible to store neatly, and pleas to do something about the lumber falls on blissfully deaf ears. Unless it's being saved for firewood, I say date it and dump it. Get a marker and mark the date the lumber entered the premises, regardless of how it got there. Six months later, go through the lumber and toss anything with a date of six months or older. A ruthless monthly culling according to date should either get the do-it-yourselfer moving on those projects, or mad as a hornet's nest. Remember that the best course of action around buzzing hornets is to stay calm. (I don't generally advocate that anybody has the right to dump someone else's clutter, so this course of action should be undertaken only when all else has failed, and it's down to the lumber goes or you go.)

Alternate storage solutions for lumber include a simple loft in your garage or an overhead step ladder storage system (this can be installed in the garage or basement). If you opt for garage, you can assume a backing-down position of going through the wood only once each year to eliminate useless scrap. In any case, the move toward solving the problem of lumber clutter can have positive results. New ideas and renewed energy might surface to propel the tinkerer toward working on an actual project involving the lumber that is currently on hand.

Magazines
(see also Desk, Mail, National Geographic)

Accumulating magazine clutter (as in piles and piles of) is the ultimate guilt trip. People keep magazines because they "have to read something in there." Having made this declaration, the magazine gets tossed into the TO READ pile, which multiplies by the dozens until there are magazines and/or trade journals all over the place. All this time, there is a little wad of guilt working on you . . ."gotta find the time to read that . . . gotta find the time to read that . . . gotta . . ." It never stops, and of course you don't have the time to read all of that stuff. Instead of admitting that, however, you hang on to the fantasy by keeping more magazines than you ever needed to know about, much less read. Everywhere you look is a reminder of your TO READ pile, which you feel compelled to do, *one day soon.* One day soon almost never rolls around, since subscriptions continue to flow into your home or office unabated; it's akin to trying to plug Hoover Dam with your pinkie.

Face it, *you're never going to catch up with all of that reading.* Only when you come to accept that undeniable fact can you organize your magazine clutter. Start by tossing out *all* magazines that are more than six months old. Don't even look at the captions on the cover or at the table of contents. If you do, you'll weaken and, convinced you *have* to read just that one article, you'll move that magazine from one pile to another pile, accomplishing absolutely nothing. Just look at the dates and start tossing.

Next, look at the remaining magazines and check for those articles that you *must* read. Cut the article out, staple it, and toss it in a TO READ basket. Now throw the rest of the magazine (mostly advertisements anyway) away. Tomorrow over coffee, pull out an article and read it. Now you've got at least a prayer of catching up. As new magazines come in, continue to scan them and clip only the articles you want to read. Keep the articles in a large basket with a pair of scissors and a stapler, and keep the basket near your favorite reading spot, be it the bed, the kitchen table, or your easy chair. When the basket gets full, throw something in the basket away (you can read it first) before you put anything else into the basket (the good old In & Out Inventory Rule at work again). You can cut down on the trauma of that decision-making process by reassessing your current subscription list. Are you getting some magazines that you've really outgrown? If so, drop the subscription. And, whatever you do, never, never, pick up a new subscription unless you let an old one go. Finally, carry some articles with you in your handbag, briefcase, or car. You never know when you're going to be stuck waiting, and twenty minutes of reading here and there puts that waiting time to good use chipping away at that guilt-grabbing monster—your TO READ pile.

Mail

(see also Announcements, Brochures, Catalogs,
Cards, Desk, Files & Filing Cabinets,
Papers, Postcards)

Mail is an amazing component of everyday life. You can't escape it. When you're young, you don't get any mail, and your life hums along quite happily without it. Sometime in your twenties, mail starts to become a constant in your life, bringing letters, bills, catalogs, magazines, and assorted charitable solicitations. As you hit your thirties, suddenly mail becomes very important, with the daily deluge of paper obligations increasing with the years. Finally, old age finds mail dwindling again, just when everybody would like to find a letter or two in the box.

At the peak of this life mail curve, clutter rears its ugly head. So much mail is coming in that you become overwhelmed. Sometimes (gasp!) you don't open the mail at all! Mail clutter, multiplying as relentlessly as the creepy pods in the *Invasion of the Bodysnatchers,* now begins to take over.

The office provides no escape. There, the mail is delivered in a cart manned by a disgustingly happy person who is obviously smiling because any minute now, the clutter will be out of the basket and onto *your* desk. Sometimes this horrific ritual takes place two or three times each day.

Mail clutter sneaks up on you when you haven't taken care of yesterday's or last week's mail. As a result, there is *no way* you will get to the mail dumped on you today. Before you know it, you've got mountains of mail everywhere — on the desk, your dining room table, top of the refrigerator, in the entry hall, and next to the bed. What are you going to do with it all, and how are you going to keep it from piling up again?

When organizing mail, the first principle is to accept the fact that if you don't do anything else with the papers, you should at least *sort* the incoming proliferation. Then, if and when you decide to actually *do* something about all that postmarked paperwork, it will be organized and waiting happily for you to work on in your usual systematic, efficient, *organized* manner.

Begin with the obvious: *open the mail.* This sounds simple enough, but as with all things simple, there's always somebody who either ignores it or does it wrong. Open the mail with a letter opener and pull the letter or bill or whatever out of the envelope. *Do not put it back in the envelope!* I see people folding and unfolding things dozens of times just so they can keep them in the envelopes they came in until they actually do something with them. This is a waste of time, and that extra outer envelope only wastes space. So remove the letter or bill, throw away its envelope and any junk inserts, and if there is a return envelope (such as those enclosed for bills), attach it to the paper (letter, or bill) with a paper clip, and lay it flat on your desk. Now might be a good time to throw away junk mail, but if you can't quite bring yourself to part with it yet, go on to the next step, which is to sort the mail into four categories.

TO DO   **TO FILE**

TO PAY   **TO READ**

Then, of course, there's the trash basket. (For more details on this paper sorting system, see *Desk*.) If you handle your mail and don't have a desk or lots of filing cabinets, you can set up your sorting station in a portable rolling basket system. The basket system can always be stored in a closet when not in use and pulled next to the bed, dining table, or your chair when you need to sort the mail or do some household paperwork. Permanent files can be stored in the closet in inexpensive transfile boxes available at office supply stores.

Whether you are working at a desk or at the dining room table, remember that sorting your mail into these four categories doesn't mean that you have "to do" it or "to pay" it or even "to file" it immediately; just sort it. Later you can do whatever it is you are supposed to do with it. The added bonus comes when you need to find something in a hurry. You won't have to sift through every piece of paper in the house or office; you will only have to go through the pile in the appropriate category. For instance, if you have a bill collector on the phone and you need to lay your hands on that unpaid bill (of course, we know you *intend* to pay it, you just haven't done so yet), all you have to do is look through the TO PAY pile, and presto, you will find it in one fourth the time it would have taken to rummage through *all* the papers.

If you're like most people, you get far more mail than you really need, but like it or not, neither rain, snow, or sleet is going to stop the influx. Eventually you have to face the music; after the mail has been sorted, it needs to be dealt with. There are things to read, items to file, and bills to pay. The TO DO basket coughs up bad news as well as good, requiring phone calls, letters, and decisions that lead to further action.

You can let your mail become a monument to clutter, or you can become its master if you'll just open it, sort it, and throw a good portion of it away the minute you get it. Deal with what's left regularly, and you'll be able to keep yourself out of the middle of the mail muddle once and for all.

CLUTTER TRAPS

As you go through your mail with an eye to action, beware of some of the more likely paper traps:

▼ **Bad News** — Bad news, whether it's a bill or a notice to appear in court, never provokes an organized response. You might do what a lot of other people do — try to ignore it. But ignoring it will not make the problem (whatever it is) go away, and the longer you wait to deal with the issue the greater your chances of compounding the problem. Consider tackling the worst first by handling the bad news, and it can only get better from that point forward.

▼ **Bills** — Bills, also known as bad news, don't go away by themselves either. Burying them in a pile and telling yourself that the bills can wait indefinitely is not a good idea. That attitude brings shut-off utilities, credit closed down at the most inopportune and embarrassing moment, and hostile calls from bill collectors. Plan to pay those bills at least once each month without fail, and you will be saving yourself more than the aggravation that goes along with past due bills.

▼ **Catalogs** — Catalogs are a real trap (for more on this, see *Catalogs*), but one of the biggest pitfalls occurs when you stop sorting or dealing with the mail, to take the time to thumb through the catalog that just came. Once you do that, it's a sure bet you won't go back to the business of the day's mail. So put the catalog in the TO READ basket and don't let it be your excuse to interrupt the job at hand — the mail.

▼ **Charity Pleas** — Charity pleas can invoke the "I really shoulds." As in, "I really should send them some money — I'll just put this over here *for now.*" That pile then grows, month after month, as, for whatever reason, you never do get around to sending that donation to that particular charity. And you know what?

That charity doesn't forget you. No siree. If you don't send them money this month, you'll hear from them again later. So give yourself a week or two to send the money (put it in the TO PAY basket) and if you don't send the money, toss it; you'll have the time and/or the cash the next time they send you a plea (which will be in the very near future).

▼ **Junk Mail** — Junk mail is a blanket term used to describe everything from charity pleas, political protest announcements, catalogs and unsolicited stickers and stamps (which are usually coupled with charity pleas). People complain about junk mail, but they can get awfully attached to it, even while they are complaining. I think junk mail should be thrown away, period. And not only that, I think you should send a form letter to the people who send you the junk mail and tell them that you are moving and you won't pay the forwarding charges, so please take your name off the list (don't forget to include the label from the junk mail — their computers have a meaningful relationship with that label that transcends anything the words of mere mortals could possibly impart). Most junk mail does not contribute to the daily quality of your life whatsoever. People can make charitable contributions, vote, and purchase consumer goods completely on their own — without the relentless prodding that arrives via junk mail. Knowing that, I don't know why more people don't put a trash can right next to the mailbox so they can drop the junk mail into the can before it ever goes in the house. No need to open it, just dump it.

Having said that, let me tell you two junk mail stories I heard at one of the classes that I teach. One fellow kept so much junk mail that his wife put her foot down and demanded that he eliminate some of the clutter it was creating. So he bought a large clothes hamper, where he *stores* the junk mail. And, you guessed it, the hamper is now full to overflowing, so he wanted to know, what should he do with all this "junk mail that probably has valuable information"? Storing mail that is termed "junk" with possible "valuable information" in a clothes hamper did not set the stage for a logical response. Throwing the stuff away was unthinkable for this gent. Someone in the class suggested that his identity was wrapped up in the junk mail and he needed it to feel important; at this point, I decided to change the subject. My guess is he went out and bought another hamper and he is loading that one up with junk mail to go with the other hamper.

Another woman in the class had saved a carload or so of junk mail magazines, newspapers, and the like. Finally she reached the heroic point where she could get rid of it. She loaded it all into her car and, bursting with civic pride, took it down to the local recycling center. At the center she was stunned to discover that the entire carload of paper, magazines, and *junk mail* had to be sorted. Envelopes with glue were unacceptable, some colored junk mail was unacceptable . . . you get the picture. By the time she had finished sorting the stuff again (she had already gone through it once before deciding to give it up in the first place), *two hours* had elapsed. The acceptable paper was weighed, and she was paid a grand total of $1.42 for her paper and her efforts. Which, in my opinion, was probably twice what the stuff was worth in the first place.

Makeup
(see Bathroom Clutter, Cosmetics)

Maps
(see also Car Accessories — Maps, *Memorabilia, Souvenirs)*

Some people keep maps from all of their trips. Then they try to stuff them into the filing cabinets, into boxes, bureau drawers, or under the bed. Other maps get used from time to time, but once unfolded, never get refolded, so they wind up a torn mess in place of what should be a map. Maintaining an inventory of maps — for sentimental reasons or otherwise — can pose a serious challenge to reason. So you still have that London subway map to remind you of your trip to London ten years ago on your anniversary? Does it take a subway map to jog those memories? Or you've got that map of Arizona from when you took the family in the RV to the Grand Canyon . . . gee, wasn't that a super trip! Yup, it sure was, but I don't see what that old battered map has to do with how great the trip was — is there a picture of the canyon on the map? If you ever do get back to London or to the Grand Canyon, you can always pick up another map either from the subway station attendant (in England) or you can visit your auto club or a local gas station prior to your trips. (And speaking of the auto club, once you've used their Trip Tiks you can ditch them, since roads and the reasons for picking any particular route change.)

Maps definitely don't equal true nostalgia, they occupy an inordinate amount of space, and are a pain in the you-know-what to keep folded. So unless you are a truck driver who criss-crosses the country in an eighteen-wheeler for a living, you can probably get by just fine without a drawer or box full of map clutter.

Memorabilia

(see also Cards, Collections, Knickknacks, Love Letters, Maps, Photographs, Postcards, Rocks, Salt & Pepper Sets, Souvenirs, Trophies, Uniforms)

According to Funk & Wagnall's *New Practical Standard Dictionary*, memorabilia is made up of "things worthy of record or an account of them." Since *worthy* seems to be the key word, a further check reveals that worthy means "deserving of respect or honor; having valuable or useful qualities." While I do think there is a place in everyone's life for memorabilia, I also know that too many people get completely carried away with this allowance and end up with crates of clutter that they pass off as valuable memorabilia. Paper memorabilia is probably the biggest offender, with love letters, postcards, children's school papers, college papers, and clippings all adding to what seems to be an ever-expanding pile of paper. You call memorabilia; everybody else calls it clutter. Add to this old uniforms, prom dresses, wedding gifts, photographs, medals, knickknacks, and trophies, and the situation quickly gets out of control.

Go through this stuff mercilessly and ask yourself if it is "deserving of respect or honor," before you decide to keep it. Be selective. If you've got photos of you in your Army uniform, you don't need to keep the uniform, especially since you'll never fit into it again in this lifetime. Ditto that prom dress. Keeping every scrap of your children's school work is ridiculous. They only care about it for about five minutes—just long enough for you to ooh and aah over it—so why should you store each spelling test for the next twenty years? Photographs can be the best records of important events, but those too can multiply far faster than necessary. Hundreds of photographs will do, thousands is pushing it. Photo nuts take pictures of absolutely everything. I've seen vacationers taking pictures of each other eating breakfast in the hotel coffee shop. How valuable is this, for goodness' sake? Don't kid yourself about your memorabilia. Ask yourself if it is valuable or worthy. If you keep lying to yourself by answering "yes," do yourself a favor; store the really valuable memorabilia in fabric-covered, metal, or plastic boxes or mount it in albums (which are particularly good for photographs, special awards, and documents and clippings). But before you start storing, get someone else in for a second opinion.

It may not be the most pleasant way to cull the mountains of memorabilia, but it works.

National Geographic

(see also Mail, Magazines)

National Geographic is a magazine in a class by itself. Whenever I walk into a house, office, or garage resplendent with walls of yellow that virtually glow in the dark, I know that I should view the scene with something akin to religious fervor. Eventually the magazine fills up every available bookshelf and the proud owner starts to pack them in boxes—for what purpose, I have no idea. Occasionally, you'll see the magazine owner trying to sell some at a garage sale. About the only interested buyers are twelve-year-old boys who are looking for pictures of naked natives.

People always try to impress upon me what a *good* magazine *National Geographic* is. Fine. It's a good magazine. Is this any reason to enshrine it in your home for perpetuity? Do you actually reread the articles on Borneo and Sumatra? Do they provide handy tips for everyday living that you refer to on a regular basis? You're going to have to bite the bullet on this one. Get rid of those back issues. A five-year collection of *National Geographic* occupies considerable space, whether on bookshelves or in cartons—and space, remember, costs money. By the time you add up the cost of keeping those magazines, along with the cost of the subscription, those walls of yellow might as well be gold. Don't waste your time and energy trying to *sell* these golden tomes either—your time is worth money too. Just give them away in one large lot (try the recycling center or a school) or (gasp) throw them away. In the end, I suppose telling you what to do with your *National Geographic* magazines is an exercise in futility. If you're the well-read owner of several shelves of that yellow glory, I know you won't pay attention to a thing I say.

Newspapers

Here's a pop quiz for you:
What are the first four letters in "newspapers"?
Gosh, you're smart. That's right:
N E W S.

Without exception, newspapers should be read immediately and tossed or recycled. Stacks of newspapers make perfect condo-miniums for bugs and are a fire hazard. Two days after the newspapers arrive, the information is not news any more. About all that paper is good for is lining the bottom of the bird cage or wrapping up garbage.

I even heard a story about a woman whose stacks of newspapers were ceiling high. One day, some stacks toppled over on her and she suffocated. I don't know if it's a true story, but it could be, and when someone dies because a stack of newspapers fell on her, I call that *news.* Knowing this (after all, you are a rational person — right?) if you *still* are worried that you're missing something in that stack of newspapers growing in the corner, try this oldie but goodie: No news is good news. Amen.

ODDS•N•ENDS (see also WHAT•CHA•MA•CALL• ITS) Miscellaneous items; various remnants and leftovers. If it's so *odd,* it's definitely time to *end* your relationship with it.

Notes
(see also Desk, Bulletin Boards, Papers)

Note nuts go around writing notes to themselves and everybody else unlucky enough to be within note range. Notes are jotted down on scrap paper, on the backs of business cards, on note pads, and on yellow legal pads. Eventually these notes are scattered all over the place, with new note pads and legal pads started by the dozens. Then, of course, you need to allocate time to organize, reevaluate, and rewrite your notes to yourself. Lordy. Give it a rest, why don'cha? Nothing much is going to get done while you're searching for notes. You'll spend twenty minutes trying to find the *right* notes, another twenty trying to decipher your handwriting, and even more time rewriting the notes. All this before any action whatsoever has been taken.

The absolute best way to deal with uncontrollable note clutter is to gather them up, and throw them away, and start clean. Then keep *one* TO DO list in one book or on one note pad, and make sure its easy to find by giving it a special spot such as a basket by the phone or a drawer near your desk. Personal reflections should be kept in a journal for your eyes only, and not be mixed in with other daily grocery and to do lists. Or you can set up a notebook that serves the sole function of holding notes. You can even divide your notebook by allocating one section for TO DO lists, one section for TO BUY lists (you might want to separate the GROCERY list out as well), one section for REMINDER lists, one section for GREAT IDEAS, and one section for PERSONAL REFLECTIONS and/or AFFIRMATIONS. Used as an addition to your daily planner or calendar, this notebook can help you keep your thoughts together so that you can act on them whenever you wish. Just remember that you have a notebook for your notes, so that the next time you find yourself reaching for a scrap of paper or a pad to make a note, you'll give your hand a little smack and use your notebook instead.

Office Supplies
(see also Calendars, Files & Filing Cabinets, Pens & Pencils, Papers)

Office supplies, from paper clips to stationery, call for a central holding station. This applies to a corporate office as well as a home office. Having supplies scattered hither and yon only makes for inaccurate inventory judgments resulting in an under- or oversupply of the items you need. Establish a cabinet or bookshelf area that will serve to hold the office supplies. If there are several people using the supplies, the storage should be as centrally located as possible.

Stationery and file supplies can be stored in their boxes. Small items, such as pens, pencils, and paper clips can be stored in clearly labeled bins. This eliminates the problem that occurs when boxes of paper clips are stacked too high, collapsing into the pens and pencils whenever someone touches the stack. With bins, you don't have to worry about collapsing stacks since the bin holds everything without requiring stacking. Whatever you do, don't assign filing-cabinet drawer space to hold office supplies. If you have no other cabinet space and have just a few items, you might be able to store them in your desk, or you can invest in a rolling basket system.

At home, this basket system can be stored in the closet and pulled out when you need to use the supplies for paying bills or answering correspondence. A dining room buffet or a section of the linen closet can also provide excellent storage for office supplies.

If you have a desk, keep a supply of stationery, pens, pencils, paper clips, rubber bands, etc. in the desk. The stationery can be kept in the file drawer in hanging file folders or on top of your desk in metal stationery trays. The smaller items can be contained neatly in your desk drawer with cutlery trays or other drawer dividers. Keep only a reasonable supply in your desk, since keeping too much in your desk can lead to clutter that actually impedes efficiency.

It is important to check all of your office supplies before you store them. Outdated rubber stamps, stationery, business cards, and other items that you never use, should be tossed out (the stationery might be cut into scratch paper). You'll save money by keeping your office supply inventory lean and mean, since cabinets full of office supply clutter often result in misplaced supplies and needlessly reordered items.

Packing Materials
(see also Boxes, Holiday Decorations)

If you ship things with some frequency, you might want to keep some packing materials on hand. But if you've got boxes, wrapping paper, bubble wrap, Styrofoam peanuts, and assorted tapes and string for the day you *might need* to pack something up—otherwise known as "might need it someday"—you need to reevaluate the cost effectiveness of your current postal service readiness. If you might need this stuff someday, and that someday rarely rolls around, you'd be better off taking that once-a-year mailing to a packing center and paying a few dollars to have it wrapped and shipped for you. It will be cheaper than storing all this stuff the rest of the year.

If, on the other hand, you do mail items with some regularity, get a tape dispenser (the kind professional movers and packers use) and store it with your rolls of tape, scissors, labels, and string, in a box or plastic sweater box, or dishpan bin. Keep a pair of scissors in the bin for that purpose only; otherwise you'll always have to spend time looking for scissors before you can begin. Paper can be stored in a box (if it's flat) or in a small round basket or trash can (if it's on a roll) in a closet or corner where you do your packing. The bubble wrap generally is on a roll and about all you can do is store it in a corner somewhere.

Styrofoam peanuts work well, but they make such a mess that it's almost not worth using them, particularly when bubble pack will do the job just as well. Boxes can be stored on a shelf inside one another, and wherever possible, broken down so that they can be stored flat either under the table or on a shelf. To reassemble them, tape them back together with strong strapping tape.

Ideally, you'll have an area where you can set up a permanent packing table, with all of your supplies either on, below, or above (on shelves) the table. You can incorporate a packing area into any other work area—around your desk, in your workshop, or in a corner of an area designated for crafts.

As with everything else, only keep what you will need in the near future. It is always simpler and cheaper to replenish your supply periodically than it is to store so many packing materials that the local shipping company's inventory pales by comparison.

PACK RAT A large, bushy-tailed rodent from the Rocky Mountains that collects and stores food and miscellaneous objects. Just like you.

Paint & Paintbrushes
(see also Art & Art Supplies, Craft Supplies)

We feel we have to keep paint and paintbrushes because, after all, that's the color we used for the den or the masterpiece we made for Grandma. And the brushes are perfectly good. There are some perfect people who always clean their paintbrushes thoroughly after using them, and who somehow manage to close the paint can properly so that the paint doesn't dry out and turn to cement. Then, of course, when these people need to paint or touch up something, it's a piece of cake.

If you are not one of these perfect people, and are more like me, this is a more likely description of your post-paint scene of the crime: You paint whatever it was that needed to be painted, which, let's face it, is *not* an exciting job. You do what you know you should always do—try to clean the brushes and close up the paint can (you still have a third of a can left after all). You rinse the brushes under a tap if the paint was water-based, or, if it was oil-based paint, you do your best with turpentine or some other nasty solvent. You can't mess with this business all day, so you give it your best shot, which in your heart you know is not good enough, and put the supposedly cleaned brushes and closed paint can away. Touch-up day rolls around (often the very next day), and you cruise over to the paint storage area and grab a brush that, as luck would have it (luck always has it this way) did *not* get clean enough, and has hardened to the consistency of a small shovel. After a day, you're probably all right with the paint—it's still usable. But don't wait more than a month or so, because if you do, you'll discover that even though you tried to close that blankety-blank can (you even used a hammer), the top perversely popped up when you weren't looking. Now the paint is hidden beneath a three-inch layer of concrete penetrable only by repeated stabs with your sharpest screwdriver. You can use that

✔️ CLUTTER CHECKLIST

To cut down on the frustration, expense, and clutter of storing painting supplies, I have instituted some policies that you might also like to incorporate.

❑ **Dump It** — Get rid of paint if: a) the lid is rusted shut; b) the label is totally obliterated, leaving the original use of the paint a mystery; and c) the stuff has fossilized to a rock-like consistency.

❑ **Low Profile** — Unless you're preparing to undertake a major painting project, don't keep more than a quart of paint on hand. You don't need more than that turning into concrete at any given time. Pour the leftover paint into a Tupperware® or other plastic container with a tight-fitting lid. Don't use metal containers, such as coffee cans, or you'll have to pick the rust out of your paint.

❑ **Extra Brush** — Always buy at least one more brush than you need. If one hardens on you, you'll have a spare, and won't have to stop and run to the store to buy another.

❑ **Hang It Up** — Hang brushes on a hook or nail. They dry a little better after you've cleaned them, and this increases your chances of being able to reuse them without having to peel them off of the surface they stuck to last.

❑ **Water-based Paint** — Always use water-based paint. If something needs oil-based paint, hire a painter or bribe a relative to do the job (which includes cleaning the brushes and closing the cans properly).

❑ **Play It Safe** — Finally, when you get rid of paint, be sure to follow environmental requirements in your area for toxic disposal. Before you toss any paint, make a note of the color and the room it was used in so you can match it later if necessary.

---

paintbrush-turned-shovel to scoop out some of the unmixed paint to glob and drip onto the wall.

Well, that's how I do it. Every time. And I have to believe I'm not alone. Admit it, paint is one category of clutter that nobody likes to deal with. The cans accumulate in the garage or basement or in some cabinet, with the contents slowly solidifying as we blissfully ignore the problem as long as possible.

In the end, the best way to keep on top of the paint problem is to follow some simple principles. First, know that ignoring the stuff is just asking for trouble. Next, get rid of the paint you never use, deal with the paint you do use properly every time you use it, and never buy more than you need in the first place. Then you'll find yourself on the road to paint clutter recovery, so that the next time you need to touch something up, you can actually do just that.

PA•PER•PHER•NA•LI•A The paper in your life, from the small scraps with scribbled phone numbers to those obnoxious computer read-outs. Paperphernalia grows in boxes, bags, drawers, and on the tops of desks, counters, and cabinets. It is often further displayed on bulletin boards and can sometimes be found stacked in obscure areas, providing housing and food for rodents and insects.

Papers

(see also Addresses, Announcements, Brochures, Bulletin Boards—
Paperphernalia, *Business Cards, Calendars, Cards, Catalogs,*
*Children—*School Papers, *College Papers, Desk, Files & Filing*
Cabinets, Love Letters, Mail, Magazines, Maps, Memorabilia,
Newspapers, Notes, Office Supplies, Phone Numbers,
Postcards, Recipes)

Paper clutter sneaks up on the mightiest of men and women. Before you can say booby hatch, papers are popping out of drawers, boxes, and bags. Piles can be seen collapsing on top of tables, desks, and refrigerators. In a futile attempt to maintain control over the ever-growing problem, the papers are stuffed into baskets, trays, and file folders, some to be lost forever. Since the daily deluge of paper somehow seems necessary to life as we know it, culling the junk papers out from the important papers can be a formidable task. Even more challenging is figuring out how to keep a piece of paper so that when we need it we can actually find the darned thing. And, given that you never look at 80 percent of the papers you file again, it is close to mind-boggling how difficult it is to manage that other 20 percent. Yet, without some sort of paper management system, daily activities can be rudely interrupted. Utilities can get turned off, credit card accounts canceled. The banker can turn you down because you couldn't find the proper documents. You have to go to court because you lost your driver's license and got a ticket while driving without that all-important piece of paper. If a spouse dies suddenly and the survivor can't lay his or her hand on documents such as the marriage certificate, the burial arrangements can be stalled, adding anguish to an already distressed situation. Lost phone numbers can mean late appointments, and misplaced notes can result in a professional set-back. All in all, paper is something that nearly everyone would probably rather do without but can't, and paper clutter just exacerbates an already bad attitude. Taken to the extreme, paperphernalia can result in paper-noia, a debilitating set of attitudes that can result in bizarre concepts, such as "paper should be piled, not filed."

For those close to, or at the point of paper-noia, organization of the paper clutter can provide the cure once and for all. A serious backlog of paper clutter does require some time in order to conquer the problem. Allocating thirty minutes here and there in an attempt to clean up two years' worth of paper accumulation never works. You'll just throw up your hands in frustration and keep on piling. So set aside a day or two and tackle the mess with determination and conviction.

PA•PER•NO•IA The affliction that comes over a person who is drowning in the daily deluge of paper.

As with all paper, the most important thing to do when it first comes into your life is to *sort* it. Most papers can be sorted into four basic categories:

TO DO   **TO FILE**

TO PAY   **TO READ**

If you're dealing with mountains of papers, get some large cardboard cartons and start sorting into them. If your paper problem isn't quite so severe, you'll want baskets on top of your desk or work table for the TO DO and TO PAY categories. Wire baskets are the best, and can be stacked on top of each other. Lucite trays that you can't really see into are not advised, since the typical paper clutterbug simply keeps adding trays to this plastic tower when existing trays are too full to deal with. Since the added trays pretty much obscure what's in the trays below, everything tends to fall into a black hole deemed permanently pending, where, of course, nothing ever happens.

For the TO FILE basket, get a large wicker basket and put it *under* your desk. Toss your filing-to-do into that basket and you'll

☑ CLUTTER CHECKLIST

Besides sorting papers immediately and filing records sensibly, these tips can help you to forestall future paper clutter and papernoia:

❑ **Decide to Decide** — Be committed to making decisions about your paperwork. Stop putting papers in piles "just for now" because you can't make a decision about what to do with them. Decide to read it, file it, pay it, or do it. Then *do it.*

❑ **Do It Now** — To ensure that you don't let your TO DO box become a burial ground, start each day by going through the box and prioritizing what needs to be done. If some of the projects are long-term ones, and especially if you find yourself procrastinating on particular projects in your box, you might have to pencil in on your calendar exactly *when* you are going to spend time on a project that you have, up to now, been avoiding. Then, *do it.*

❑ **Junk the Junk** — Scan the junk mail as soon as it arrives and then do what you should be doing with junk — throw it away. Why do you think they call it junk mail?

❑ **Purge Pending** — Don't keep a pending file or basket. Things plopped into this file or bin either become lost or happily forgotten forever. Something you think of as "pending" is actually something that needs to be done sooner or later. Therefore, it goes in the TO DO box, where it won't be forgotten since you'll see it every time you work on the papers in that box.

❑ **Out in the Open** — Never keep any work in progress inside your desk drawers. All work in progress should go into the TO DO or TO PAY baskets or in the special project cart or area. Thus, work not yet finished won't become buried (or lost) in a drawer somewhere and you will be able to tell at a glance the amount of work yet to be done or the status of work currently in progress. (See illustration at right.)

❑ **Traveling Companion** — Organize your briefcase with the same four-step paper sorting process. Make file folders for TO DO, TO PAY, TO FILE, and TO READ. As materials accumulate that are going to be transported by briefcase, instead of throwing the papers in a pile in the briefcase, put them into the appropriate file. You'll be able to deal with the material in a more organized manner while traveling and when you get back to the office. Keep some essentials in the case: a box of paper clips, pens, a small stapler, scissors, and Scotch tape. Whether you are on the commuter train or at home, you can organize your paperwork as easily as if you were at your desk. When you return to your office, it's easy to transfer the materials in those briefcase files into the proper basket at any work stations.

❑ **Don't Be a Copy Cat**—Resist the urge to copy everything you have on paper. Only copy papers that actually *require* duplication, such as legal or financial paperwork that's being sent out. Every time you copy something on a duplicating machine, you're contributing to the blizzard of papers blanketing the human race.

❑ **Tomorrow Is a New Day**—Finally, make sure you spend ten to fifteen minutes at the end of each day tidying up your work area. It helps to clear your head a bit when you put everything in its place once each day. When you hit the paper decks the following day, you'll feel that you are making a fresh start on your paperwork and the day.

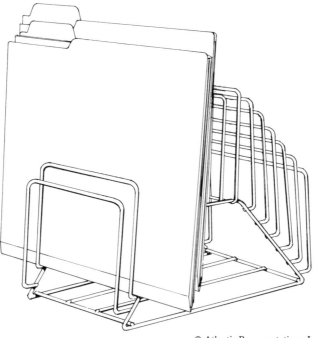

© Atlantic Representations, Inc.

stop picking it up twenty times a day as you move papers around, muttering, "Oh yes, I need to file that—later."

Your TO READ basket should be behind or beside your work area. Toss all magazines, newspapers, and newsletters in that basket to read later.

The final sorting category for papers is the TRASH BASKET. I strongly recommend it as a simple solution to an ugly problem. With that recommendation comes a promise; I promise you that fully 50 percent of paper can be tossed and never missed. And a good portion of that paper, such as bills, announcements, and junk mail by the ton, will be right back on your doorstep in next week's or next month's mail. Trust me, those people will not forget you.

When it comes to trash baskets, buy a large one. Get rid of any dinky, prissy little wastebaskets that scream FULL after two or three pieces of junk mail and a couple of wadded up pieces of paper. Keep this large trash basket next to your desk or work area, and if you want to be really clever, put one right outside or inside the door. Then when you bring the mail in the house, you dump a lot of it before it ever has a chance to become part of the paper clutter.

You can have other categories if you like. CALLS TO MAKE can be a good division for some, and catalog junkies feel compelled to have a TO BUY section. However you choose to do it, *do it,* and then keep the papers confined either to those baskets or to your storage or filing system. Whatever you do, use the KISS Rule: Keep It Simple, Stupid.

Once you've sorted the papers, you'll have to do something with them, of course. Set up your filing system according to the guidelines in *Files & Filing Cabinets.* Hints on managing your TO READ basket can be gleaned by checking the *Books, Magazines, National Geographic,* and *Newspapers* sections. The rest of the papers in either your TO DO or TO PAY baskets could include just about anything from ADDRESSES to POSTCARDS. As you sift through those baskets, check the appropriate category in this book to pick up some methods for handling that particular piece of paper.

CLUTTER TRAPS

You may feel like you've created a paper skyscraper, but you've got nothing on the government. According to the *Los Angeles Times,* although military services and defense contractors continue to fight the tide of paper, with each F-18 jet fuselage that is turned out, 16,295 pages of manufacturing paperwork is created. Since the F-18 program began, it has generated enough paper to equal the height of the Empire State Building.

If your paperwork is threatening to bury you alive, it's time to tear down your personal paper skyscraper. Along with the categories of paper already handled elsewhere in this book (which includes *Addresses, Announcements, Brochures, Bulletin Boards —* Paperphernalia, *Business Cards, Calendars, Cards, Catalogs, Children —* School Papers, *College Papers, Desk —* contents, *Files & Filing Cabinets, Love Letters, Mail, Magazines, Maps, Memorabilia, Newspapers, Notes, Office Supplies, Phone Numbers, Postcards, and Recipes*) here are some other possible paper traps you might eliminate:

▼ **Articles** — Articles get cut out because they are interesting, funny, or in perfect alignment with our own brilliant thought processes. They get saved even though they are never read again. They even get (horrors!) photocopied and mailed to other people so they can share our thrill with these words of wisdom. Eventually, they get filed, where they, quite simply, rot. I say read it and weep. Or laugh. Or congratulate yourself on agreeing with the writer. Whatever. Then throw it away.

▼ **Bank Statements** — Some people keep bank statements on five different accounts for twenty-five years. The last I heard, the government wasn't requiring that much financial information for tax purposes, but check with your accountant to find out how long you should keep bank statements that cover tax-deductible financial transactions.

Those statements that must be saved should be kept in their envelopes with the checks. Mark the month and year on the front of the envelope and store the whole business for the year in a plastic sweater box which can be put on a shelf, in a cabinet, or under the bed. My bookkeeper hates this concept. She, like lots of other people, thinks the thing to do is to remove the statement and store it flat in a file folder. The checks are then pulled out and sorted into categories by disbursement. I think that's asking for trouble. I'd lose some checks for sure, and since you almost never have to go back to statements or checks anyway unless there's a problem, why go to all that extra effort? Pick your own poison here.

▼ **Bills** — Ideally, bills should be paid when they come in. If this were done, they wouldn't pile up and become lost or ignored with disastrous results. Unfortunately, many people don't have the luxury of paying bills the minute they arrive due to limited cash flow. Not only that, it's much more efficient to group tasks, so that you would pay five bills at once, rather than stopping five different times during the week to gather up the paperwork to pay each bill.

Nevertheless, it's important to open the bills when they arrive. Throw out the junk inserts, clip the envelope to the bill (do *not* put the bill back into the envelope) and put the bill in the TO PAY basket. At least once every two weeks, check your TO PAY basket by checking *all* of the bills and paying what you can, what is due or overdue, or what is the most critical (such as the utilities). Once the bill is paid, mark the date paid and the check number on your portion of the stub, and file it with your paid bills, with the most recently paid bill on top.

▼ **Cartoons** — Cartoon clippers like to think that their sense of humor is inherently superior to others. Clipped cartoons confirm that idea, and as the clippers file (or pile) said cartoons, lots of smug thoughts go through their heads. What they don't stop to consider though, is that once that cartoon lands in a pile or a file, it's a dead duck. Nobody else will ever see it or know about the cartoon, and if nobody else knows about the cartoon, they'll never know what a sense of humor you have. So, either post the cartoons in a scrapbook for everyone to enjoy, put them under the glass on your desk (and *not* tacked to the wall or stuck on the refrigerator), or stick them in with your correspondence to give the recipient a chuckle along with your words of wisdom. Whatever you do, don't file them. If it comes to that, you might just as well throw them away. The results are the same — you'll never see them again.

▼ **Correspondence** — It is not, contrary to popular belief, necessary to keep *all* correspondence. Cover letters, stupid letters, and letters asking for money for causes you don't believe in can be instantly tossed. Letters with hopelessly out-of-date information can also be given the heave-ho. Old love letters are fun to keep, but you don't need to keep a trunk full — a shoe box full will definitely do.

Keep some family correspondence as memorabilia, and, unless the letters contain important family information and/or records, toss the rest away. Only keep Great Grandpa's letters to his relatives if they are relative to you and your family or if they serve as a record of the family history.

Keep the correspondence that needs to be kept for sentimental, legal, or accounting purposes by category in either files, baskets, or transfile boxes. A ruthless culling of letters as they are opened can keep these pieces of paper from contributing to your other paper clutter.

▼ **Important Documents** — Believe it or not, you can get rid of some "important" documents. Before you worry about how to store your important papers, go through them and toss all expired insurance policies, product warranties, and passports. Documents on automobiles that you no longer own can also go. Pedigree papers on pets that have passed away can be parted with. In short, if the document has expired, get rid of it. The remaining relevant documents such as birth certificates, deeds, stock certificates, and insurance policies are best kept in a fireproof filing cabinet or box. File them neatly in the metal box or cabinet, and make sure someone else knows where they are in case something happens to you.

▼ **Meeting Records** — Anyone who is a member of a Board of Directors, serves on a committee, or attends regular group business meetings, has a much better than average chance of being inundated (not to mention intimidated) by the avalanche of papers that is invariably passed out at each meeting. The distribution includes information on upcoming events, schedules, budgets, agendas, minutes, and committee reports, just to name a few possibilities. Since everything is relevant, the papers do need to be kept for reference for a certain period of time, but keeping them in file folders never works, since the documents are often referred to at future meetings (and you can't very well cart a dozen file folders to each meeting). Because of this, records of meetings, be they Board of Directors, fund raising event, committee, or other business meetings, need to be kept in a chronological order.

Along with minutes and notes, meetings often generate other pieces of pertinent backup material. All of these papers can easily be kept intact in chronological order in a three-ring binder divided by months or meeting dates. If you leave the Board, or after the charitable event has been successfully concluded, you can pass this complete set of records over to the next person in one large but simple and organized binder.

▼ **Phone Messages** — Phone messages are noted on scraps of paper, pink telephone message slips, call record slips, and Post-It™ notes. These pieces of paper then disappear in the other paper clutter, often resurfacing woefully after the fact — too late to make the necessary call back. Cut down on the scattered messages by establishing a phone message center where all phone messages can be dropped. This can be a box, basket, or bin placed near the phone. Ask everyone to drop the messages there (as opposed to say, sticking them to your chair). Have messages put in that spot only. Then it's a breeze for one and all to check the message center on their way in or out of the house or office.

▼ **Special Projects** — Special projects frequently generate too much paper to hold in a TO DO basket. These ongoing projects (such as lawsuits, writing projects, research projects) need to be organized and easily accessible on a daily basis. A rolling basket system can handle the job exceptionally well, with the project paperwork broken down into manageable segments and stored in the hanging file system on top of the baskets. The baskets under the files can hold either supplies or incoming and outgoing paperwork pertaining to the project. When the project is complete, remove the manila files and place them directly into transfile boxes or the filing cabinet for permanent storage. A credenza, bookcase, or table behind your desk can also serve as a staging/holding area for these projects, so long as they are neatly and categorically stacked.

Pens & Pencils
(see also Desk, Office Supplies)

Keeping pens and pencils is an automatic reflex action. Throwing dead pens and pencils away is a thought that somehow escapes even the most brilliant among us. Knowing how difficult this concept can be for some, I would still like to yell my views across the room: The next time you pull out a pen or pencil that doesn't write, DON'T PUT IT BACK. THROW IT AWAY!!! The rest — and you don't need a gross — can be kept in one tray in a desk drawer and/or a container on the desk. The container should be roomy and simple. A glass jar that lets you see your selection clearly is better than some fancy opaque gizmo that you have to struggle with to get at your favorite pen. You can also keep spare pens and pencils in one other special area — a drawer or a cigar box will do nicely. If you work the crossword puzzle every day, make sure you've got some working pens or sharp pencils in a container next to your easy chair, the bed, or the kitchen table. Near every phone, place a container of pens and pencils, along with note paper for immediate access when you need those items most. Once you've mastered the art of controlling pen and pencil clutter, you'll be surprised how it can make your life easier on a daily basis. The next time somebody says, "Quick, grab a pen and write this down," you'll be able to do just that.

Pet Paraphernalia

Pets enrich our lives by giving us unconditional love. This love is accompanied by clutter that involves leashes, flea powders, brushes, and mongo bags of food that Fido likes to tip over or gnaw at so that the food trickles out of a burst bottom corner. There are also

---

✔️ CLUTTER CHECKLIST

Since it is unrealistic to think that the essentials that go into the care and feeding of our precious pets can be tossed, here are a few ideas about how you can organize the basics:

❑ **Hooks** — Put the leashes on a hook next to the door or just inside a closet.

❑ **Trash Cans** — Put large bags of dog food, bird seed, or cat litter into a covered trash can.

❑ **Supply Caddy** — Keep brushes, grooming gloves, and flea powders all together in a plastic supply caddy. When you're ready to brush and powder, simply cart everything to the designated pet grooming area. Medicines and ointments can also be kept in a supply caddy or a plastic shoe box so that they are separate from human medicines.

❑ **Records** — Pet records should be kept in a file folder or large envelope with your other papers, so you can find them if you need them.

❑ **Quality Time** — Keep Kitty's brush next to your easy chair or your favorite outdoor lounge chair. When Kitty rubs up against your legs, just reach for the brush, and get ready for some immediate purr-fection.

---

ointments and medicines and vaccination and other paper records that need to be put somewhere.

Organizing the pet gear starts with establishing a holding area for the items—from food to toys to leashes. You can put it on the service porch or in a corner in the kitchen, just so long as you put as much of it in one area as possible. Keep everything current by weeding out old medications or dried shampoos, and get rid of toys and combs that Kitty or Fido hates. Make creative use of hooks and clutter containers to hold everything, keep the pet paraphernalia limited to the essentials, and you'll be able to conquer your pet's clutter with ease. Meow.

Phone Numbers

(see also Business Cards, Bulletin Boards, Papers)

Phone numbers and addresses enter our lives via any number of avenues. Scraps of paper, business cards, and personal mail—all carry important phone numbers and addresses needed for future reference. Almost everyone has lost an important phone number or misplaced a vital address at one time or another. To eliminate the frantic scramble for a misplaced phone number or address, keep your phone numbers on a Rolodex that's large enough to accommodate your needs.

Some people keep all of their phone numbers in an address book. This only works if changes and additions are rarely made. Otherwise, the address book turns into an unreadable mess, with names and numbers scratched out, and new entries squeezed in along the side of the page. A Rolodex system eliminates this confusion, since it is easy to add names and make changes by inserting a new card in the proper alphabetical order. There are all types of these Rolodex systems available, small and large (some are even fairly attractive), to suit almost anyone's phone number needs.

As you collect phone numbers (whether it's via business cards or tiny scraps of papers that you hastily scribble information on), throw them into a small basket or container. Periodically, you (or someone else) can sit down and type up the cards for the Rolodex. You can also staple business cards directly to the Rolodex card. If the business card is a bit too big, trim a piece off of the top or bottom of the card, and save yourself the work of typing or writing the information onto the Rolodex card. If you need to scrounge up a number before it gets transferred to the Rolodex, you'll know it isn't lost. It will be in the basket waiting to be transferred to the Rolodex. This system for your phone numbers and addresses can work wonders for your daily professional life, and it might just perk up your social life as well!

Photographs
(see also Collections, Heirlooms, Memorabilia, Souvenirs)

Clutterbugs take to photographs like bees to honey. They run around snapping pictures of everything from Grandpa's seventieth birthday party to the new bushes in the back yard. They're addicted to cameras. The finger that pushes the button starts to twitch if it doesn't get to click-click a camera every time you turn around. These people have pictures up the proverbial wazoo. If you, too, are drowning in photographs, consider this organizing axiom: *Photographs don't do anybody any good if they can't be seen.*

Of course everybody *plans* to put their zillions of photographs in an album (or two or three or twenty albums), but they never do. I once met a woman who put her photos into albums the minute she brought them home from the developers (she had sixty albums). I was so thunderstruck at the thought that someone could actually be *that* efficient that all I could say to the woman was, "Aren't you wonderful?" Most people don't do that (I certainly don't!), and so, naturally, the photos don't get seen, much less enjoyed. If you've got about sixty albums worth of photos lying all over the place (and stuffed in closets and drawers), begin by dragging them out, one bag or box at a time, and looking at them. Then follow the guidelines in the Clutter Checklist to bring order out of chaos.

Plaques
(see Souvenirs, Trophies)

Postcards
(see also Bulletin Boards, Cards, Collections, Desk, Mail, Memorabilia, Papers, Souvenirs)

For some mysterious reason, we feel compelled to keep postcards that are sent to us from friends and relatives. If they went to the trouble of sending this card from Europe, we should keep it, and besides that, there's a picture of the Eiffel Tower on the card. Gotta save it, right? Wrong. Read it and toss it. If you want to see the Eiffel Tower again, save your money and take your own trip.

✒ CLUTTER CHECKLIST

❏ **Declare a Moratorium**—If you've got several years of un-sorted photos, spend ninety minutes each week working on the project. Don't take any more pictures until you have organized the backlog you already have!

❏ **Preserve the Past**—Old family heirloom photos deserve priority since, left untended, they can deteriorate badly. You'll also want to check with family members for missing information about the people in the photos so that you can record that information on or with the photo.

❏ **Critics Corner**—Look at your photos critically, with an eye to eliminate all but the best. Get rid of shots that are blurred or fuzzy. Toss those unflattering shots that make you cringe every time you look at them. Also consider getting rid of those photos that are dumb, boring, or mediocre (you don't need a shot of Dad talking to Mom). Definitely get rid of pictures of people that you no longer recognize.

❏ **Dump the Dupes**—Throw or give away duplicate photographs.

❏ **Label, Label, If You're Able**—Mark photos with the date and a number. Put the same date and number on the corresponding negative with a fine India ink pen. Store the negatives in an envelope and mark the dates and numbers on the front of the envelopes. This is a lot of work, and there's no point in doing it if you are fairly certain you'll never make reprints. If you think reprints are unnecessary, it's not a sin to toss the negatives.

❏ **Categorize**—As you're editing your photos, you may want to organize them by category. For example, *Vacations, Special Events, Pets, Sports, Family*. You can also make chronological cat-

Posters

Posters very often are a reflection of the phases that we pass through politically, emotionally, and artistically. We pick them up, intending to "do something with this great poster," and nine times out of ten, that stinker gets rolled up, stuck under the bed or in a closet, and winds up being pitifully squished and crumpled as we pile other junk on top of it. If you have managed to survive adolescence and the

egories according to periods of your life, such as *Childhood, College,* or *New York, California* (for the time you lived in each of those places).

❑ **Storage** — Once the photos are organized you can store them in large manila envelopes or plastic shoe or sweater boxes with labels. If you put photos in albums, be sure to put the albums where everyone can go through them whenever they want. You might also consider framing special photos and hanging them on the wall, or making a collage of your shots and hanging it.

❑ **Slide Shows** — Sort your slides just as ruthlessly as you would photos, using the same sorting principles. You can also sort them into slide "shows" and store each show in a carrousel tray with a label (i.e., Amy's Eighth Birthday). Slide trays or carrousels can be stored on shelves or on a closet floor, or in a cabinet where you have a bit of extra space. If you have a lot of slides you might want to purchase a cabinet to keep them all stored neatly in that one space.

❑ **Instant Documentation** — Finally, and perhaps most important, when you bring the photos home, make sure you immediately identify the photo by noting who is in the photo, the location, and the year, as well as ages of people (such as children). You may think you will always remember all of the details of those photos, but you won't. The day will undoubtedly come when you find yourself holding up a photo in total bewilderment, wondering who on earth that person with the red hair is. Durned if I know. You won't know either fifteen years from now, so if you don't do anything else to organize your photos, at least start identifying them now so you won't be so befuddled later on.

ten or so perilous years that follow, you may have passed through your poster phase.

If so, get rid of the ones that are either smashed or hanging forlornly in the garage by giving them to someone younger or throwing them out. And, it goes without saying that if you're going to buy posters, the first thing you should do when you get them home is get them up on the wall. If you're not prepared to do that, don't buy them in the first place. .

Pots & Pans
(see also Appliances, Dishes, Kitchen Utensils)

There's never enough room in the kitchen—or so it seems—for the pots and pans. They're stacked in an unmanageable heap (sometimes along-side small appliances) on the one or two available shelves in the lower cabinet. Getting to the big stew pot means bending over to pull out the skillets first, followed by unloading all of the pans that are stacked within the big stew pot. That done, the pans and skillets go back into the cupboard—but only temporarily. Because after you use and wash the stew pot, you've got to repeat this process, taking the skillets and pans out, restacking the pans inside the stew pot, putting it back into the cupboard, followed by the skillets. No wonder the cook is cranky.

First, get rid of all of those old pots and pans that you've been hoarding for twenty years and now never use. Ditto those fancy gourmet pans and molds that you never use. And if you do use the molds only once or twice a year, store them in a remote cupboard (such as the one over the refrigerator) so that they don't clutter up the everyday cookware inventory.

Whether you are a gourmet chef, a fast-food cook for the troops, or a noncook who prepares food only to survive, having organized pots and pans can reduce the aggravation that can accompany the culinary process, and cleanup is a bit easier as well. After all, creative cooking is an art, but it can be tough to be artistic when your "studio" looks like a disaster zone. Organizing the pots and pans could very easily put a little joy back into your cooking and your kitchen.

Purse
(see Handbags)

Recipes
(see also Books—Cookbooks)

Recipes come into our lives through cookbooks, magazines, and newspapers. Cookbooks are easy to deal with if you only buy books that you intend to use, and then put them on a shelf rather than on the counter where they just get in the way. Recipes that you clip from magazines and newspapers are another matter. And the time-honored, much-loved recipes from Grandma and your mother-in-law only add to the recipe clutter. The first commandment of recipes is that unless you are going to put your clipped recipes *in order,* and

✔️ CLUTTER CHECKLIST

The clatter and din, and the inconvenience that goes along with these piles of pots and pans, can be reduced with the following space-saving tips:

❑ **Climb the Wall** — Use any available wall space by installing a pegboard with hooks. You can hang your pots, pans, large utensils, potholders, and the like on this pegboard. Put up the pots and pans that you use most often. Since they'll be washed frequently, they won't suffer from grease or dirt buildup.

❑ **Let It Hang** — Install a pot rack that hangs down from the ceiling to hold your pots and pans. Chefs in restaurants and hotels often have their cooking equipment hanging from this rack over or near the cooking areas for easy fuss-free access and storage.

❑ **Pull-outs** — Convert your cabinet shelves into pull-out shelves that are modified drawers. Most new homes now feature these for cookware storage. (See illustration below.)

❑ **Vertical Storage** — Baking pans, trays, and platters can be stored in the cupboard vertically by adding plywood dividers to separate and hold the items in a standing, organized position.

❑ **Put a Lid on It** — Pan lids can be stored separately in a drawer, on hooks on the wall, or inside the cupboard. Inside the cabinet, you can store them on a lid storage rack. This same rack can be placed on a shelf near the stove and your hanging pots and pans.

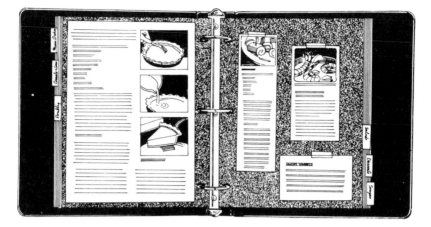

then follow that up by actually *using* those recipes on a fairly regular basis, *don't clip the buggers in the first place.* If you do, that one bulging drawer of yellowing, never used recipes will multiply to two or three drawers you could be using to store something that you *use.*

For those recipes that you *do* want to use, you can make your own personal cookbook. Buy a large three-ring binder (get the type that sales people use for display and presentation purposes). This binder is encased in plastic so that sales people can slip a piece of paper with information onto the front of the binder. It's going to allow *you* to keep the thing clean. Next, buy a box of clear plastic sheet protectors. Both the binders and sheet protectors are available at your office supply store. Organize your recipes by category, such as *Breads, Entrees, Appetizers, Desserts,* etc. Then slip each recipe into a sheet protector and staple or tape it to the black piece of paper inside the plastic. If your recipes are written on two sides of the paper or an index card, simply remove the black insert sheet from inside the plastic sheet protector and staple the recipe to the plastic. All you have to do is flip the sheet protector over to see the rest of the recipe. This binder makes it easy for you to keep the photos of the recipe *with* the recipe—even if you have to use two pages. Just put the picture on the left side, and the corresponding recipe on the right side. No more losing the picture and wondering why you ever saved the recipe in the first place. (You saved it because it looked delicious in the picture, remember?) Use index dividers (also available at the stationery store) to divide your categories. You now have your own customized cookbook that can be expanded at any time (or weeded out) and can also be kept clean. It's simple to add recipes to the proper category, and if you wish, you can snap one of the sheet protectors out of the binder and work from that one easy-to-clean page, thus eliminating the need to have the bulky books on the counter while you are cooking. If your collection is extensive, you might want to have separate binders for different categories. Any way you look at it, this book takes care of all recipes, whether they're on scraps of paper or an entire magazine page. No more recopying onto those stupid little index cards (that always get lost) or shoving clippings into boxes and drawers. With this book, it will be a snap to hone your culinary talents, and they will be remembered with pleasure by all who are lucky enough to taste the results of your latest recipe test. Everyone will be asking *you* for your wonderful recipe, which you can keep secret in your personal cookbook, or can easily share by flipping to the correct page in the book for easy photocopying.

Rocks
(see also Collections, Memorabilia, Souvenirs)

Most people keep rocks to add to a collection or because they picked them up as a souvenir (like that rock you stubbed your toe on at Lake Michigan last summer). Either way, rocks are clutter. Consider the dusting consequences. How many rocks do you need anyway? What possible purpose can a rock serve? Here are the only things I think you can do with a rock:

- Use it as a paperweight
- Use it as a doorstop
- Put it in the garden
- Put it in the fish tank
- Rock 'n' roll with one
- Stone your obnoxious neighbor

That's it. I can't think of another good reason to keep a rock.

Salt & Pepper Sets
(see also Collections, Dishes, Knickknacks, Memorabilia, Souvenirs)

Three sets of salt and pepper shakers is about all any family needs. One set goes with the good china. One set goes on the table for everyday use. And one set stays in the kitchen for cooking. More than that means you're into collecting the things, and, as collections go, this is one of the worst when it comes to maintenance. Those itty bitty holes get clogged up with grime and dust that is a royal pain to clean, and displaying them is tough. Why would you put ten sets of salt and pepper shakers in the living room? Or bedroom? Or bathroom? That leaves the dining room or the kitchen. Nobody *ever* has extra room in the kitchen, so that's out. That leaves the dining room and a hutch or some shelves up around the molding on the walls. Most people need hutch space for good china, and shelves on the wall just make the room look smaller, and increases the housekeeping load. Nope, I still say three sets, max. With salt and pepper *in* them.

School Papers
(see College Papers, Children — Papers)

Sewing Supplies
(see also Craft Supplies)

It's all too easy for sewing supplies to take up as much as a room's worth of space — that's why people have "sewing rooms," I guess. But unless you really are serious about sewing, there's no reason to keep dozens of zippers, ribbons, trims, buttons, threads, patterns, and fabric scraps of every description and size. If you are just a mender, keep only the basics — thread, seam ripper, needles, buttons, and a few snaps. These should be kept with a pair of sewing scissors in a compartmentalized sewing basket which keeps everything neat. Procrastinating menders, beware. If you've got piles of clothes accumulating in bags and boxes that you're going to get to "someday," it's time to take drastic action. Start fresh by taking *everything* to your local tailor or seamstress. Then, as new mending projects pop up, take ten or fifteen minutes in the evening to sew on that one button or fix that hem rather than waiting for it to pile up.

Serious sewers tell themselves that they need a complete inventory of everything from bobbins to zippers. This is only valid if you really do use that fabric or zipper before the year is out. If you find yourself consistently going past the same piece of fabric or never looking at a pattern after the first time you use it, it's time to unload the excess by giving it to friends, relatives, or charity. You'll be more productive with your current sewing projects if you don't have to constantly dig past stuff you don't intend to use anyway. The sewing notions you keep because you know you'll use them can be stored in organized sewing baskets or plastic shoe boxes with labels. These boxes stack neatly on shelves or on the floor, and you can see at a glance how many zippers, for example, are in the zipper box.

Patterns never fit back into the envelope once they've been

unfolded, but there is a simple way to store them so that they can be used again. Put the patterns into a 9 x 12 manila envelope. Cut the pattern envelope open, and attach it to the front of the envelope, and your patterns will stay organized and easy to use when you need them.

If you've got a lot of fabric, chances are it is in large (hopefully) folded pieces, on rolls, or in scrap piles. Fabric is like everything else — if you're not using it, and know deep down that you won't use it, you should give it away — now. Fabric on rolls is often kept for that upholstery project that you'll get to someday. Today is as good a someday as any other, so what are you waiting for? I believe that scraps should be used, turned into rags, given to a quilting society, or tossed. You'll need an awfully good reason to continue allocating precious storage space for those bits and pieces. Those scraps that you just can't part with can be stored, folded, in large zip-lock storage bags. This helps keep them organized and makes it easier to sort through them. (A heap of scraps gets wrinkled and annoys you when you have to dig through them.) If zip-lock bags seem like too much trouble, keep one large bag or box of scraps, but when it gets full, throw some away before you add any more to the pile. Fabric on rolls can be covered in plastic and stored under the bed or upright in a round small plastic trash can. Large pieces of fabric can be folded around a piece of cardboard and stored in a box under the bed or on a shelf, and smaller pieces can be put in plastic sweater bags or boxes and stored on a shelf or under the bed as well. You can hang fabric over hangers if you've got space in the closet. Look for string pricing tabs — check your stationery store or a store that supplies retailers — to hang on the fabric hangers. Note the yardage and the date on the tag and hook it on the hanger. You can attach the tags to folded pieces with a pin, so that you will always know how much yardage you have to work with.

Sewing supplies can take over, and when that happens, you're faced with clutter rather than useful supplies. So *use it* or *lose it.*

Shoes & Boots
(see also Clothes)

There are mountains in every state in the country. These mountains are called Shoe Mountains. Shoe mountains spring forth seemingly unaided, from the floors of otherwise normal closet floor space. Platform shoes left over from the sixties mate happily with dressy spikes from the seventies. Sneakers, designer and otherwise, defy organization. Shoes that need repair, that haven't been worn in years, that hurt your feet, and that are just plain ugly, are haphazardly mingling with perfectly good shoes that you paid perfectly good money for, and that you do wear on a fairly regular basis. Once again, clearing up this particular type of clutter begins with getting rid of things. Get rid of the shoes if:

- •They are uncomfortable and hurt your feet or back;
- •You're only keeping them because you paid a lot of money for them;
- •They are hopelessly out of date and out of style;
- •They don't go with anything you wear, so you never wear them.

Next, gather up any shoes that need to be repaired and take them to the shoe shop immediately. Now you are left with the shoes that make a meaningful contribution to your life by providing comfort and style for your feet.

Remember, your shoes are supposed to make your feet happy. If you put on a pair of shoes or boots that don't give you happy feet, give them to some feet that will smile to see them coming.

Shopping Bags
(see also Bags)

Keeping shopping bags makes only a shade more sense than keeping plastic and paper bags. Collecting those makes *no* sense. It's true that a shopping bag is handy enough, and invites reuse. It's also true that they almost never get reused unless it's to hold other clutter. Thus, shopping bags full of papers, clothes, and other serious whatnot can be found stuffed into corners and closets all over the house. Canvas shopping bags can be a good idea—you never know when you'll have to tote something somewhere, and the bag could be the answer. But one or two canvas bags should suit you. Since you only have two arms and two hands, by my mathematical reckoning, you can only tote two canvas bags comfortably at any one time. Not only that, if you have more than two canvas bags, you'll start using them to store clutter. So keep a couple of canvas tote bags, and, if you must, keep a couple of paper bags. But more than those few bags won't be productive; indeed, they are a clutter trap just waiting to happen.

Socks & Stockings
(see also Clothes)

I'm not altogether certain that there is a way to keep socks and stockings organized. But you can keep the clutter down by

✔ CLUTTER CHECKLIST

Here are a few techniques for making the most of your shoe storage in your available closet space:

❑ **Shoe Rack** — Put all your shoes on a shoe rack that hangs over the inside of the closet or bedroom door or one that sits on the closet floor. The metal racks are far and away the best shoe holders. They are sturdy and give you a look at your choices for footwear at a glance.

❑ **Shoe Bags** — Hanging shoe bags serve the same purpose as the racks and can be hung on the inside or back of a door.

❑ **Shoe Boxes** — Plastic shoe boxes can hold shoes and be stacked on the floor or on shelves. You can stack dressy shoes near your dressy clothes and casual shoes near your sporty attire.

❑ **Shoe Cubbies** — Built-in shoe cubicles provide a compartment for each pair of shoes.

❑ **Boot Trees** — Put boot trees inside your boots and they can be kept neatly either on the floor or on a shelf.

❑ **Boot Center** — You can establish a boot center during the times boots are frequently worn by staking out a corner inside the back door (or front door if you have an apartment). Put a large plastic dishpan in the corner so that galoshes can be immediately removed and put into the pan for drying. If you've got several family members trucking in and out, consider installing some low shelves near the entry for the tubs. This way the boots are where they should be at all times — near the door, ready to put on feet that are ready to walk out into the elements.

immediately throwing away stockings that have runs and tossing socks with no mate. Socks with no mate deserve pity, but not hope. Hoping that the missing sock will turn up is futile after about six weeks. Give it up. Either throw the single sock out or make a toy for the dog with it (dogs love to pull on knotted panty hose too — with you tugging at the other end). Likewise, it's tempting to throw a pair of stockings with a small run back into the drawer. Trouble is, when you need to look your absolute best, you'll grab for the stockings and find nothing but runs — and even a small run won't do for this particular occasion. Also, a small run turns into a big run the minute you stretch the stockings over your legs.

Socks and stocking storage can be kept a bit neater by dividing the drawer for categories. You can put two shoe boxes inside the drawer and put light-colored socks or stockings in one and dark-colored ones in the other, or you can store your stockings in a hanging stocking bag.

These bags have pockets for stocking storage — one pair to a pocket — and can be hung in the closet or on a hook. You can put small children's socks in a bin on the floor of the closet next to their shoes, making it easier for them to get dressed and keep their things organized. Periodically check your supply of socks and stockings so that you can purchase what you need *before* you run out. You should always have one pair of unopened stockings on hand for that special occasion. Once you open that package, make a note to buy at least one new pair. Don't wait until you are completely out to run to the store (on the way to work or to an event). Don't wait until your tennis socks are so stretched out that they are falling down around your ankles, either. Stock up and replenish your supply before you have to, and your feet and your life will be sweeter indeed.

Souvenirs

(see also Collections, Gifts, Knickknacks, Maps, Memorabilia, Photographs, Postcards, Rocks, Salt & Pepper Sets, Stuffed Animals, Trophies, Uniforms)

For the real meaning of souvenirs, the word *junk* pops immediately to mind. Because, let's face it, most souvenirs are junk. It's over-priced and poorly made junk at that, and although these items seem exciting while we're on a trip, the excitement starts to wane considerably when you have to cart all the stuffed animals, figurines, commemorative plaques, and goofy hats back home. Once you get them home, where on earth do you put the darned things? In the dining room? Living room? Bedroom? Out of room? Try the bathroom. At least then you can relax in your bath and stare with dazed eyeballs at your collection of vacation junk.

Along with the commemorative spoons, plastic statues, and corny bumper stickers will be the zillions of photographs and postcards that you picked up. Talk about redundant. If you have photographs and postcards of the Empire State Building or Disneyland, why do you need a plastic statue and a stuffed Mickey Mouse? If you *must* buy souvenirs, at least go for useful merchandise. An overpriced T-shirt is far better than an overpriced made-in-Japan doodad. You can wear the T-shirt to death, and it shouldn't be too much of a problem to get it home in the first place. If it's your habit to run around buying souvenirs for your friends and relatives, why don't you set a new trend. Your friends and relatives don't need another ridiculous bauble to remind them of *your* trip. They know you went away. It's punishment enough to make them look at your slides and photos. If you can't bring yourself to return empty-handed, bring T-shirts. At least the recipient can work in the yard or sleep in the thing. If you've got souvenirs from past forays packed away or stuffed in the back of the closet, get rid of them and give yourself some newfound space. I'd tell you to give them away, but in the case of souvenirs, I'm afraid you won't find any takers.

Spices

Spices clutter up the cupboards, with small and large tins and bottles vying for what little space there is in the first place. Reaching for a spice in the back of the cupboard means knocking down several of the spices in the front. Cooks in a hurry tend to put the spices that are most often used in the front, and conveniently forget everything behind the front row. Those spices in the back lose their flavor and, worse than that, turn buggy. The bugs that get into spices are so tiny that you can easily miss them. And since you probably shake the spice right out into the food anyway, you won't ever see the bugs because they jump directly into the sauce to do the backstroke without your ever knowing it. Yummy. If you haven't used a particular spice for a long time, and can't think when you will, get rid of it. Then purchase spices carefully. If you buy an exotic spice for a special one-time-only dish, get the smallest possible amount so that if you have to throw the rest of it away six months later you won't feel so bad about it.

The spices that are kept and used regularly should be stored in alphabetical order. If you are the only one who cooks and you really know your spices by category, you can group them that way (i.e.,

celery seed, poppy seed, and sesame seed would be one group).

You can store them on turntables in the cupboard nearest the stove, or you can install a narrow shelf under your upper cabinets and over the counter. Since spices require minimal depth for storage, this shouldn't interfere with your counter space. You can also install a shelf or two on the wall near the stove. Traditional spice racks that you purchase can help, but often they don't accommodate all the different sizes and shapes of the tins and bottles, so if you want to buy one, make sure it will hold round glass jars as well as oblong tins. Another solution — and one builders are now including in new kitchens — is to turn a drawer near the stove into a spice section. This is done by making a step-like insert and putting it into the drawer. The spices are then laid down into the drawer, with the steps providing support and division for the spices. And, if you've got a pantry, you can always consider installing a door rack to hold some of your spices and oils. However you do it, the primary consideration should be what spices you really *need* and *use.* Having fifty different spices in the cupboard that never get used does not a gourmet cook make.

Sports Equipment
(see also Balls, Children, Exercise Equipment)

Sports equipment tends to get jammed into closets, corners, basements, and garages. Then when you need something, even though you've got sports gear scattered everywhere, you can't find the one thing you need. You have to sort through hockey sticks, baseball bats, tennis rackets. Balls, including basketballs, baseballs, golf balls, and tennis balls are never where they should be, and it always requires at least a fifteen minute search before you find the one you need. Protective gear invariably gets separated, leaving you with one knee pad and three elbow pads when what you need is two knee pads. The only thing to do is be a sport and streamline your sports storage equipment.

First, get rid of anything you no longer use. If your kid's Babe Ruth days are long past, give that baseball equipment to a child just entering that phase. If you broke your leg the last time you skied and swore you'd never ski again, get rid of the skis and take up something less adventurous.

The equipment that you use with some regularity should be stored in one area, such as a corner in the basement, garage, hallway, or in a closet, even if it is out of season. A lot of things can be mounted on a wall, from skis to bicycles, so if you've got wall space—like in the garage—this is a good way to go. The rafters in a garage can hold out-of-season skis as well. A large trash can will accommodate balls and bats. Tennis rackets can be hung on hooks on a pegboard system on the wall, and special protective gear like kneepads and catcher's masks can be stored in a drawer, a large rubber bin, a chest, or a foot locker. Once you've established a "sports center" it's a simple matter to find what you need and to put the equipment away when you're finished with it. Wails of despair over misplaced equipment should be reduced substantially, and you will find yourself with much more control over the clutter.

> **STUFF** Generally possessions, especially household goods; a collection of things without value; trash, materials, equipment or supplies used in various activities; personal property; belongings; an accumulation of matter. Or, the clutter that you absolutely refuse to let go of, and that you feel obligated to protect, as in, "Get away from my *stuff!*"

Stuffed Animals
(see also Baby Clothes, Children, Collections, Toys)

Stuffed animals are usually an adult problem. Generally, children outgrow their stuffed animals and, except for one or two favorites, don't even notice when the collection is given or thrown away. It's the parents, especially mothers, who have a hard time giving up those oh-so-darling critters. If your kid is sixteen and you're still hanging on to that tattered bear and cute rabbit, it's time to let go. Take photos of the animals if you need to keep the vision alive, but then bundle all of them up and take them to charity.

If your child is still at an age where stuffed animals are important, try limiting the acquisitions. The child probably favors a special few animals anyway, and buying more just because you think they are cute won't guarantee that the child will agree with your assessment. What it does guarantee is that you will be adding to the clutter. If other people have contributed to the problem with gifts of stuffed animals, teach the kids charity by having them select the animals they don't play with and take them together to the local charity. When new animals come in the door, you can pick out some old ones that the child doesn't like and give them away. The rest can be organized by picking out a chosen few for the bed and putting the rest in a special wicker trunk or on a shelf. Finally, if your kid is twenty-one years old and away at college, but has left you as guardian of the collection, pack all of the stuffed animals up and ship them directly to the proud owner. After all, if the animals are important enough to keep, they should be kept on the owner's bed, not yours. In the end, a corral cluttered with outgrown stuffed animals won't keep either you or your child perpetually young.

Suitcases

People keep suitcases forever, figuring that they'll need them someday, most likely to move. Since most people don't move all that often, owning more than a few suitcases just means moving and storing more clutter. If you do move, you can use boxes or wardrobe boxes for a lot of your clothes. Your clothes get wrinkled in boxes (except maybe for the wardrobe boxes) and they get wrinkled in suitcases, so why do you need suitcases to move? Use boxes, then throw them away, and give yourself a lot of extra storage space. Keep enough suitcases to handle your traveling needs, and no more. Since most travel doesn't require more than two suitcases and a carry-on, limit yourself to that, and keep only those suitcases that are in good repair. Add a garment bag, and unless you routinely travel with an entourage, I can't imagine that you will need more than that in the way of luggage.

Luggage can be stored under the stairs, under the bed, and on shelves in closets that are inaccessible for daily use. If you have a trunk or foot locker, you might be able to store some of your suitcases inside them. Soft-sided luggage is ideal for storage, since it's easily folded or flattened. You can even store the soft-sided luggage inside other luggage, so that, while it may look like you only have one suitcase in the closet, in reality you have three (two are stored inside the largest suitcase). Be realistic about your traveling needs and you won't have to concern yourself with suitcases cluttering the place. Bon voyage.

Ties
(see also Clothes, Gifts)

Unfortunately, when it comes to gifts for men, ties top the list of possibilities. Consequently, Dad ends up with more ties than any human could ever hope to wear. To stem the tide of ties, make your gift wishes known. People are not mind readers, so let them know that you'd really love a copy of that book on golf or something snazzy for the car. Rather have a new bush for the yard than another tie? Let people know this. And if you're in a spot trying to figure out what to get that all-important man and all you can come up with is ties, try to be more creative. Give a gift of your time by treating him to a special dinner out or through services (you'll pay someone to do yardwork for two months). Or come right out and ask him what he wants. A simple, "If you don't tell me what you want, you're getting a tie" should do the trick. Those tips should take care of future tie clutter.

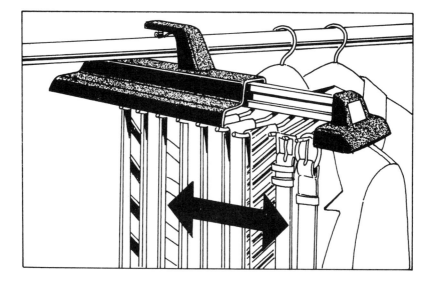

Current tie clutter can be alleviated by eliminating those horrible ties that you never wore and won't wear. Put the remaining ties on a tie rack (there are several new types in the stores to choose from). If you don't want a fandangled tie rack, you can install a curtain rod on the back of the bedroom door, and can hang your ties there. A handful of ties is all the average man ever needs, and if somebody insists that dozens of ties are necessary to look good, remind all within earshot that these ties can only go around one neck — one at a time. A little common sense goes a long way with ties.

Tools

(see also Electrical Supplies, Gardening Equipment
& Supplies, Hardware)

Tools are one of the little necessities of life. Even if all you ever plan to do is hang a picture or two or assemble something, you need the basics — hammer, screwdriver, and a pair of pliers. If that's all you've got, you're in great shape — no clutter there. But most people start with those three tools, and somehow the tools multiply unceasingly until you've got everything from a saw to that fabulous thingamajig that comes complete with fifteen different bits, pieces, and accessories. You've got all this great stuff, but where is the blankety-blank hammer when you need it? You'll have no trouble locating the hammer if you establish a tool center (even if it's only a drawer or a corner in the closet), and if you get rid of tools that are rusted, broken, or too much trouble to use.

Essential tools can be stored in a number of ways. A conventional tool box can do the trick, as can a metal parts cabinet. If you've got

only a few items, you can store them in a sturdy shoe box or a plastic kitty litter box on a shelf or under the bed. If you're more of a Mr. or Mrs. Fixit and have room in the garage or basement, establish a tool center in one corner, and set up a work table there if possible. Many tools can be hung on the wall from a pegboard and hook system or with nails. To ensure that the tools fit back on the wall easily, you can make an outline of the tool directly onto the wall so that it's easy for anyone to replace the tools properly. A locked cabinet is best for storing tools if there are small children about, and you can separate the tools easily enough by putting all of the screwdrivers into a coffee can, for instance. When it comes to tools, safety and usefulness are the key factors to consider for organization and storage. Only put useful tools into your tool center, and store them safely and sensibly, and you'll be able to get a grip on the tool clutter problem and have what you need when you need it.

Toys

(see also Car Accessories & Supplies—Toys, Children, Games, Gifts, Stuffed Animals)

Keeping up with toy clutter can be the biggest daily organizational challenge of all. The kids scatter toys from one end of the house to the other, and when it comes time to pick them all up and put them away, the little darlings are nowhere to be found and you end up with the thankless chore. The crux of the problem is the *number* of toys kids have today. Kids today could set up their own toy stores, they have so much stuff. In my day, kids got books from the library and new toys on their birthday, at Christmas, and when Grandma came to visit. This system kept the toy accumulation down to a reasonable level, and while we still cluttered the place up when we played, I don't think there was nearly the mess people are faced with today. I don't believe in showering kids with an unending stream of toys, but if you must do that, at least apply the In & Out Inventory Rule. When a new toy comes in, an old one goes out. Period. Kids lose interest in older toys quickly, and by continuously weeding out those unwanted toys, the inventory (and therefore the clutter) can be managed somewhat. Not only that, you can teach your children responsibility by letting them pick out what they no longer want to play with and helping you give those items to charity.

That said, the question still remains—how can those remaining toys be organized? The first thing *not* to do is to get a toy box. All of the toys get piled into a toy box, and when the child wants something from the toy box, you guessed it, everything comes out

to get to the desired toy, usually at the bottom of the box. A better
system is to group toys first. Books, dolls, blocks, soldiers, etc. can
be grouped and stored in plastic or rubber bins. Kitty litter pans,
dishpans, baskets, and toy cages on wheels can all be used to hold
specific groups of items.

To help the child keep the categories straight, try taping a picture
of, say, an animal (for stuffed animals) to the front of the bin or
cage, or a flashcard with the category (such as *Games*). Or label it
with a marker so that the toys go back into the proper bin. This will
keep things organized, and teach your child some organizational
skills as well.

The bins can be placed on shelves, under the bed, or on the closet
floor. A wicker trunk can hold extra stuffed animals, and books for
younger children can do better standing upright in a bin than on a
bookshelf. The child can flip through the books in a bin—on the
bookshelf all they can see is the spine, which discourages reading.
If kids do try to find a book, they'll pull an entire shelf of books
down to find what they want, since the picture on the *front* of the
books is what sells the child on the idea of reading. To facilitate

end-of-the-day toy clutter cleanup, have the child put all of the toys into a toy cage on wheels and roll it back to their room to be put in the proper bin category later. A laundry basket can also handle this duty. The child can throw all of the toys into the basket, take it to his or her room, and distribute the toys into the bins. You might want to keep a toy cage or laundry basket handy in the rooms where the clutter tends to accumulate (such as the family room). It only takes a few seconds to toss everything into the basket, versus carrying the toys a few at a time back to the bedroom. And when you are carrying that laundry basket full of toys into the bedroom to join the countless other toys, make a mental note to yourself. The next time you are near a toy store, take a detour. Every toy that enters the house means more clutter in your life, so you have no one but yourself to blame if you keep contributing to the problem by buying yet another one.

TRASH Something with little or no value; substandard or worthless; something broken or crumbled; garbage. Or, what you think of your spouse's stuff and what your spouse thinks of your stuff.

Trays
(see Pots & Pans)

Trophies
(see also Memorabilia, Souvenirs)

Trophies and plaques are concrete evidence that we were, at some point in time, incredibly talented. Ribbons and award citations add to the proof. Trouble is, where do we display this stuff so that everybody knows that we won the Pee Wee League championship game thirty years ago, and that ten years later we got a ribbon for the best fruit jam at the county fair? I don't know who gives a hoot about that fame or your jam, but if you can't part with your bonafide memorial ornament, at least don't pack it away. After all, what's a trophy or award for, if not to show off? Put the trophies on a shelf or in a case. Ribbons can be placed in a scrapbook by sliding them into plastic sleeves (available at stationery stores) and putting them in a three-ring binder. Big-shot awards and plaques go on the wall, of course, for maximum impressive effect. When guests drop by, you can act nonchalant as they peruse your many awards out of the corners of their eyes. But before you get too carried away with these testaments to your talents, consider this: One definition of the word "trophy" listed in Funk & Wagnall's *New Practical Standard Dictionary* is "Anything taken from an enemy and displayed or treasured in proof of victory."

Uniforms
(see also Closets, Clothes, Memorabilia)

Childhood uniforms such as Cub Scout, Girl Scout, and Little League tend to get packed away when they're outgrown, where they join the adult military uniforms which, unfortunately, are also outgrown. And the simple truth is that once these outfits have been outgrown, both mentally and physically, it is a rare occasion that the owners can shrink back into these memorable articles of clothing. Packing these clothes away only does the moths good, so it might be time to give up the ghost of what was but is no more. Children's uniforms can be passed along (either personally or through charitable outlets) to other children who can use these outfits *now*, and military uniforms can be sold to a clothing resale shop that deals in eccentric clothing, or can be given to a child for dress-up or Halloween. You can even give a military jacket to a surly teenager and there's a good shot that he'll wear it with his other rebellious clothes and think he looks cool. Letting go of these items can be easier than you think. Just consider how happy someone else will be to strut your stuff, and hand it over.

Vacuum Cleaner Attachments

Vacuum cleaner parts tend to get separated from the vacuum cleaner, and when you need that special gizmo attachment so you clean some corner or crevice, you can't find the attachment. Round up all of your attachments, and make certain that what you have goes with your current vacuum cleaner. If you've got parts that went with a discarded vacuum, throw them away. They might be good attachments, but without the vacuum cleaner they are useless, so get rid of them. The remaining attachments can be stored in a bag hung near the vacuum cleaner, or in a bin (such as a dishpan or kitty litter pan) kept on a shelf near the vacuum. A shallow pan with parts can also be stored under the bed if space is limited. And if you are keeping exotic attachments that you know you will never use, get rid of them. Vacuuming is a chore, not an art, and chores are tedious enough without surrounding the necessary equipment with a lot of unnecessary clutter.

Vases
(see also Dishes, Gifts)

Receiving flowers is a wonderful thing. We accept them in the spirit with which they were given, then we admire them, display them, and watch them eventually die. Once they're expired, we throw the dead flowers out, wash the vase, and then try to figure out what to do with it because, after all, it's still perfectly good. Sooner or later you find yourself with many vases (especially if you were ever in the hospital) and no place to put them. And when company comes, do you haul these vases out to put flowers in? Nope. You use your good crystal vase. Those other vases get stored and moved from place to place. Every garage sale I go to has a selection of vases for sale. Even at rock-bottom prices (ten ¢) these things don't go. I say get rid of them when you get rid of the flowers. If you can't find anybody to give them to, throw them out. If you can't bear tossing them all out, keep one but make it purposeful. Throw pennies into it and start a savings account with the accumulated funds.

Videotapes

VCR programming has ushered in a new era of clutter—videotapes. People fall right into a clutter trap when they start videotaping middle-of-the-night movies, the shows that are on when you aren't home, and programs that are on opposite the program you really are watching (are you still with me here?). On top of that, people buy music videos, kiddie videos, exercise videos, and movie videos. Once you start doing this, you'll increase your video inventory until those tapes are coming out of your ears. I met a guy in one of my classes who had hundreds of backed up, waiting-to-be-watched videos. He was consumed with trying to find the time to catch up on all of this vid-idiot business, and he came to my class hoping to find the magic answer. Unfortunately the answer is that nobody has that much time (especially when you consider that the guy was probably taping new stuff while he was catching up on the old taped stuff) and I suggested he give up his video habit, which was cluttering up his time and his house. If you've got the video bug, you might want to start by cutting back on your automatic impulse to program another show onto videotape. Then, keep some Post-it™ notes with your videos, and when you tape something, put a Post-it™ with the name of the program on the tape (this eliminates having to play a video to see what's on it). After that, you can store your videos on a video rack (portable ones can be purchased at variety or stereo shops) or you can store them in plastic sweater boxes, near the TV. But the best thing you can do is cut back on your habit by only keeping two or three videos on hand at any given time. That way, if you haven't watched what was previously taped, you'll just tape over it when something else you want to see comes along.

Wallets
(see also Gifts, Handbags)

Wallets are like eyeglasses—when we are tired of them or they wear out, we buy a newer, more fashionable wallet, but we don't get rid of the old wallet that served us so long and so well. Add to that the fact that wallets are commonly given as gifts, and you're likely to have a drawer full of wallets. Since almost nobody ever uses more than one wallet at a time, and since wallets don't get switched according to outfit as purses do, there's no reason to keep extra wallets. None. If you had wanted to use it, you wouldn't have switched in the first place. Keep a spare if you must, but get rid of the rest. Check them all for money that you may have left behind in the secret compartment (people are often pleasantly surprised to find a stash of a few extra dollars that they had forgotten about) and give the empty wallets to charity. Or, you could leave some money *in* the wallet for charity, since what charities need more than anything else is *cash.*

Wine
(see also Gifts)

Wine is another gift trap, created when well-meaning friends hand us a bottle for holidays or dinners. While we graciously accept the bottle, there's usually more in the kitchen, and a surplus results. Unless you have a wine cellar, what to do with a dozen bottles of wine can be a critical storage problem. People who live in tiny apartments are particularly plagued by the wine storage problem. The best thing to do is stop saving it for that "special occasion" that may or may not ever occur. Recycle the stuff. The next time you go to someone's house for dinner, grab a bottle of your in-house stock and take it with you. Ditto birthdays of acquaintances—grab another bottle to present. The acquaintance probably didn't expect a gift since you aren't close friends, so they'll be impressed with your thoughtfulness. If you've got dozens of bottles you'd like to unload, look for a charity that is having an event, and donate the wine to them for a tax deduction. Put the bottles that you keep in a wine rack that can be mounted on a wall, set on a bookcase or inside (or on top of) a cabinet, or set directly on the floor, depending on the size you get. Crates can be divided with plywood (if you're handy), and stacked with wine bottles stored inside (on their sides, not upright). While you're figuring out how to store your wine inventory, don't forget that your next special occasion can be sooner than you think. Like tonight, for example. A quiet dinner by yourself or with a friend calls for a glass of wine every bit as much as a birthday or holiday. And still another special occasion is to give up drinking altogether, in which case, you'll give it all away.

Wives

Technically, wives, like husbands, are not really clutter. But they can be the source of clutter in nearly every room in the house. Makeup and other beauty paraphernalia chokes the bathroom until the clutter (and the husband) is totally out of control. Wives accept the kids' clutter (macaroni art, school papers, and paper plate greeting cards), and without thinking, start stacking and pinning the stuff all over the house. Clothes closets become crammed beyond belief, until gradually the wife usurps most of the space that was allocated for her dearly beloved's clothes. All of this drives husbands crazy, and it's remarkable that they say so little about it. Of course some never say anything until the day they walk out, leaving the wife with her clutter to keep her company. A more sensible and loving solution to the problem might be for the husband to implement the Yours, Mine, and Ours Rule to combat his other half's clutter (see *Husbands*). Another terrific solution is to cough up the money to have a professional come in and help clear up the clutter—but this only works if the wife is ready to do some clutterbusting. All things considered, the vows were for better or worse, and if clutter is as bad as it gets, at least there's a cure.

ZE•RO The absence of portion; naught; nothing. Or, the sign that you've gone too far in de-junking. Everyone needs a little clutter in their lives, after all.

Clutterbusters to Live By

Conquering clutter can be an ongoing process. Even after you've heroically cleared away the clutter, it manages to creep back into your life. Along with the Ten Commandments on Clutter, these clutterbusters are a quick review of the principles of clutter control and should help you keep your head above water when you start to feel like you're drowning in the daily deluge of clutter:

▼ Stop saying that you'll need it "someday." Someday is here already.

▼ Just because something is "still perfectly good" doesn't mean it isn't meaningless clutter. Give it away if you don't use it, but don't keep storing it just because it's still good.

▼ If you've packed it, you're not using it. If you're not using it, it's time to lose it.

▼ If you are storing things for other people, it's time to serve notice. Call them and tell them to come get their stuff. What are you, a moving and storage company?

▼ Don't use storage units as a dumping ground for clutter that you don't know what to do with.

▼ Remember how much it costs to keep clutter; what's your square footage going for these days?

▼ Ask yourself how much time you want to spend next week, next month, and next year, cleaning and caring for your clutter.

▼ Once you've decided to give something away, get rid of it immediately; otherwise you'll change your mind later and keep it.

▼ Do the worst first, and it will be downhill from there.

▼ If the clutter seems overwhelming, remember that "inch by inch, it's a cinch." Some areas can be tackled in segments. If you spend one hour each day working on your tax receipts, at the end of the week you will have contributed six or seven hours to the project and will hopefully be finished.

▼ Don't accept interruptions or distractions when you are getting organized; you'll never get done if you keep answering the phone or looking through the catalogs you come across.

▼ Establish staging areas for specific purposes. Keep a small table near the door and *always* keep your keys and handbag there.

▼ Group like items together and keep them in clutter containers to minimize the scatter effect of out-of-control clutter.

▼ Keep items as close to their point of use as possible.

▼ Don't buy anything unless you've got a place to put it.

▼ Use the KISS Rule. Keep it Simple, Stupid.

▼ Spend a few minutes every day picking up the clutter.

▼ Put things away, right away. Stop saying you'll just "put it over here, *for now*." For now turns into forever, and before you know it, you've got clutter up to your eyebrows.

▼ Get rid of clothes that are too small, out of date, or so boring you haven't worn them for years.

▼ Don't buy clothes just because they are on sale.

▼ Don't put clothes that need to be mended or cleaned back into the closet. Mend them, clean them, or get rid of them.

▼ Don't buy clothing that requires lots of special care.

▼ Get rid of shoes that hurt your feet or back.

▼ Throw away worn out and unmated socks and stockings with runs in them.

▼ Do the laundry before it piles up; put it away immediately.

▼ Keep a basket in the laundry area for items that are ill-fitting, out of date, or just plain not wanted any more. Then take them to your favorite charity.

▼ Stop overloading your handbag.

▼ Don't hang on to all of your children's baby things forever. Someone needs them more than you do.

▼ Make children take care of their own clutter—*all* of it. They might get tired of the chore and decide to give a few unwanted toys away to reduce their housekeeping burden.

▼ Don't buy your kids any new toys unless they get rid of some old ones.

▼ Don't buy your kids toys every three minutes to begin with. They don't need it, and neither do you.

▼ If you're not using or enjoying your heirlooms now, give them to a relative who will use and enjoy them.

▼ Get rid of gadgets and gizmos that are more mysterious than useful to you.

▼ Give up appliances that are broken or that you never use.

▼ Stop hoarding paper and plastic bags.

▼ Get rid of duplicates such as spatulas, corkscrews, and can openers.

▼ Don't hang on to spices you never use.

▼ Keep recipes in a recipe binder instead of a kitchen drawer.

▼ Throw away keys that don't belong to anything.

▼ Spend as much time putting photos into albums as you do taking them.

▼ Only keep road maps you use with some regularity.

▼ If you're not exercising with your exercise equipment, get rid of it, and get yourself on a walking program which doesn't require any equipment.

▼ Only tackle one arts and crafts project at a time, and finish it before you go on to the next project.

▼ Clear out old cosmetics regularly; they harbor bacteria and only contribute to the clutter crisis.

▼ Open and sort your mail as soon as you get it.

▼ Junk the junk mail immediately.

▼ Keep a large trash basket near your desk or work area.

▼ Sort your papers into the Four-Step Paper System: TO DO, TO PAY, TO FILE, and TO READ. Throw the rest away.

▼ Set up the Four-Step Paper System in your briefcase.

▼ When you receive an invitation or announcement of an opening, enter the date on the calendar at once, and throw the papers (except the directions) away.

▼ Keep a calendar near the phone; also carry one with you.

▼ Stop hanging on to calendars just because you like the pictures.

▼ Throw away pens that don't write.

▼ Keep pens and paper by the phone so anyone who answers the phone can take a message and place it in a "message center."

▼ Keep phone numbers in a basket; put them on a Rolodex later.

▼ Throw newspapers away immediately.

▼ Clip magazine articles you need, and throw the rest of the magazine away.

▼ Don't hang on to every issue of *National Geographic*.

▼ Give your books away when you have finished reading them.

▼ Don't hang on to catalogs for longer than sixty days.

▼ Limit the number of subscriptions you receive.

▼ Don't use a bulletin board; it will only turn into a hanging burial ground.

▼ Get rid of misprinted stationery and outdated rubber stamps.

▼ Keep your notes contained in a notebook or binder.

▼ Use binders to organize special papers from special projects.

▼ Keep office supplies in a central area; don't use your filing cabinet as a supply storage cabinet.

▼ Don't color code your filing system. You don't need extra work.

▼ Never remove the hanging file folder from the filing cabinet; it is there to permanently mark your place and eliminate misfiling the manila folder that fits inside the hanging folder.

▼ Remember that 80 percent of everything you file you never look at again, so stop saving every article and scrap of paper you come across.

▼ Never keep work in progress inside your desk drawers.

▼ Carry postcards with you so you can catch up on personal correspondence during waiting time.

▼ Take a few minutes at the end of each day to tidy up your work area.

▼ Cut back on your collecting.

▼ Collecting often just means accumulating. Remember that, as you go about adding to your collection of clutter.

▼ Let people know you don't want any more knickknacks for gifts.

▼ Don't keep memorabilia unless it has serious emotional or financial value to you.

▼ Stop buying souvenirs and silly gifts.

▼ Only buy furniture that is functional as well as decorative.

▼ If you have more than one junk drawer, you have too many. Start cleaning the junk drawers out while talking on the telephone and keep at it until you've stemmed the clutter tide.

▼ Let other people help you by delegating chores or hiring professional help. Stop saying that it's easier to do it yourself. If it's so easy, why haven't you done it already?

▼ Don't use your garage as a dumping ground. You are only postponing the day of reckoning.

▼ When you find yourself running out of room, forget about moving; just stop and spend time weeding out the clutter. A good de-junking every six months or so can keep you in control of your space and your clutter.

Well there it is. Everything you ever wanted to know about clutter, and then some. Or is it? If you've got a clutter problem that I didn't cover, or if you've got a nifty solution to a special type of clutter, I'd love to hear from you. In the meantime, if you start to feel overwhelmed by your clutter, remember that clutter, so long as it is not a state of mind, is easily dispensed with. Knowing that, my thoughts and good wishes are with you as you set about conquering your clutter.

Much Success!

Send your problems or solutions for clutter to:
Stephanie Culp
THE ORGANIZATION
P.O. Box 890700
Temecula, CA 92589-0700

It's Your Turn: Answers to Commonly Asked Questions

Whether you decide to conquer your clutter on your own or with the help of a professional, you may still have some questions about the process of getting organized. Here are the answers to some commonly asked questions that may help you get started, keep going, and then stay organized and clutter-free:

> *"I'm really a very clean person, so I don't understand why I can't handle this clutter. If I'm so clean, shouldn't I be organized as well?"*

Not necessarily. Clean is not the same as organized. If you don't believe me, check your dictionary. The talent and wherewithal required to scrub a toilet is not the same as that required to cull through clutter and organize and store what you need. Cleanliness is a mighty fine thing. Some people even say it is next to godliness. That may be, but it still won't buy you a ticket to heaven, and it also won't get you organized. You won't hear me trying to tell anybody how to clean and beware of cleaning experts who try to tell you how to get organized. If you are lucky enough to have someone else do your cleaning and you can't understand why they can't deal with the clutter, the answer is simple enough. They clean. Shifting clutter around does not, as a general rule, make for a meaningful experience for a cleaning person, just as scrubbing the floor or toilet bowl does not motivate the organizer. If you like to clean but hate to organize, you may need to hire a professional organizer to help you with the backlog of clutter. This lets you continue to keep a clean and (newly) organized house with as little effort and agony as possible.

> *"Everything is so out of control, I don't know where to start."*

Start in a room, but just *start*. And don't stop until that room is done—even if it takes several days in a row. Then go right on to the next room and work yourself around your house or office. (In your office you may want to start with your desk, then do the filing cabinets.) The main thing to remember is to tackle the clutter in big pieces so you are gradually creating a place for everything. Cleaning out a shelf here and there never works; the minute you walk away, the clutter creeps back onto the shelf. You need to organize the entire closet, cupboard, and room in order to make meaningful progress in your clutter-control campaign.

"How long will it take to conquer my clutter?"

This question is impossible to answer because it depends on two very important factors: the amount of clutter in your life, and your attitude. If you have twelve years' worth of paper clutter, your problem won't be cleared up overnight. If you spend ten minutes agonizing over every scrap of paper, trying to decide if you should keep it or not, your attitude will add enormous amounts of time to the project. And if you hide clutter from others as well as yourself (like those mysterious boxes under the bed), only to dig them out as a surprise addition of "more things to go through," you will be equally surprised at the extra time it takes to deal with those boxes. Be realistic about the length of time it could take. Twelve years' worth of clutter might take two weeks to organize; if you are an agonizer, it might take two months. In the end, your clutter-control project will take exactly as long as you do, based on the number of years' worth of accumulation.

"Why can't my secretary/assistant keep all the papers in my office perfectly organized?"

First of all, good secretaries are not exactly growing on trees these days, so you might want to begin by making sure you really do have a good secretary. Once you've done that and you're satisfied you have a good assistant, take a hard look at your habits. Are you refusing to delegate? Are you hoarding, stacking, stashing, and spreading papers in, on, and around your desk? Is the filing system supervised by one person, or are there several people digging around in those drawers every day? For that matter, do you even *have* a system for people to follow? Take a good look at that paper in your workplace. If those papers are getting bogged down as they move from point A to point B, your secretary may not be at fault. Most likely, you need to put an organized paper-pushing system into place, and then make sure everybody follows that system, including you.

"How do I know if I need to hire a professional organizer to help me get organized?"

You know you need help if you've tried several times to get control over your clutter and, despite your best efforts and good intentions, have failed to conquer the clutter in your life. You know you need help when you admit you need help. And you know you need help if there is no possible way for you to set aside the time required to do the job yourself.

"How can an outsider possibly understand my stuff well enough to help me organize it?"

Certain organizational principles apply to nearly every situation (those have been discussed in this book). Along with those principles, a good professional organizer will work with you to tailor your clutter-control system to suit your particular professional and personal lifestyles.

"I'm too embarrassed to get help. Nobody's as bad as me and my mess. I don't know what to do."

First, stop worrying about comparing your problem to other people. Instead, focus on *solving* the problem. Fussing about what others think or say won't fix the problem. If you're going to ask for help, don't call in a friend or relative. Nine times out of ten, they can't possibly keep their negative judgmental comments to themselves, and you'll only feel worse and probably give up prematurely. Either resolve to set aside the time to do it yourself and then commit completely to that, or hire a good professional organizer. Once a professional organizer has been in business for a few years, they've seen it all. Unless somebody has called the Health Department on you, chances are the organizer won't bat an eye at your clutter.

"How do I know if a professional organizer is qualified to do the job I need to have done?"

The same way you know if any professional service is qualified. Ask for references. Ask the organizer how long she or he has been in business. Find out what kind of projects he has done, and if she specializes in any particular area. Discuss any budgetary restraints you may have to be sure you have a good financial fit.

Make sure that the professional can work with you on a mutually agreeable schedule to meet your organizational goals. A good professional organizer will work with you to solve your problem and will be available to help you in the future should the need arise (hopefully it won't). A good professional organizer is never judgmental and always offers the assurance of complete confidentiality. Remember that organizing is a very personalized service, so make sure you feel comfortable about the person who will be helping you. Don't be afraid to shop around.

> *"What guarantee is there that once I get organized, I'll keep everything organized?"*

There is no guarantee. That's entirely up to you. If you set up a simple system to suit your lifestyle and make use of the principles and simple tips in this book, it should be easy for you to stay on top of your clutter. After that it's up to you to stop procrastinating, stashing, spreading, messing, and hoarding the clutter that comes into your life. Only you can put an end once and for all to your days as a clutterbug or pack rat.

Storage: Clutter Containers

Once you've eliminated unnecessary clutter, you'll need to store what's left. Here are some clutter containers that can help you store what you can't bear to part with. You'll find them in your local department store, variety stores, hardware stores, catalogs, and specialty closet stores.

ADD-A-SHELF — These instant shelves are made of coated wire or sometimes particle board. Put them in cabinets or closets and you have an instant additional shelf. These work in kitchen cabinets (for dishes), in linen closets (use a clip-on basket type of add-a-shelf to hold placemats) and in clothes closets, where they increase shelf space to hold more sweaters, T-shirts, hats, or other items commonly stored on closet shelves.

ARCHITECT'S BINS — These are containers that are divided to hold tall standing items (like rolled architectural plans). You can store anything that's long in them, from baseball bats to fishing poles to curtain rods.

BASKETS — Wicker and wire baskets can be used to hold everything from papers to craft supplies. Toys, magazines, cosmetics, postcards, stationery, craft supplies, and stuffed animals are but a few of the things that can be stored in baskets. Baskets with lids can be an ideal clutter container inside a cabinet or on a shelf or dresser top. Attractive, useful, and often inexpensive, baskets can serve as clutter containers in the house or office.

BINS — Bins of all sizes can hold all manner of things, from electrical supplies to toys. Usually made of plastic or rubber, they can organize certain categories of clutter and be stored on shelves, in cabinets, under the bed, or on the closet floor.

BLANKET STORAGE BOX — Made of vinyl and plastic, this box is made to hold out-of-season blankets, but can also hold bulky sweaters or other knitted goods. Add some cedar chips to keep the moths away. This box sits nicely on a top closet shelf or corner, keeping your winter things in good order until you are ready to use them again.

CANRACK™ — Kitchens that have little or no space to store canned goods can benefit from this item, which stores cans horizontally, one behind the other. This allows the storage of canned goods in cabinets that would have been too short.

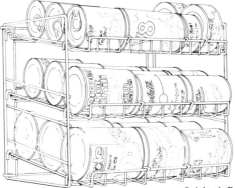

© Atlantic Representations, Inc.

CAR CLIP — This gadget attaches to the dashboard of the car and holds notes for your convenience. Clip directions to your destination there, or use it to hold your schedule of things to do for the day, keeping it immediately available for reference as you are out and about.

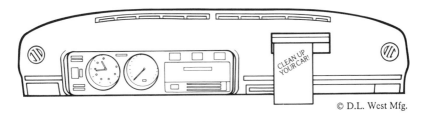

© D.L. West Mfg.

CAR MAP CASE — This case holds maps neatly, and provides a central storage envelope for the maps that you might need to keep in the car all the time. It makes controlling map clutter a simple matter, and can eliminate the mess and confusion an unfolded map can create in the car.

CAR ORGANIZER — This plastic and vinyl hanging bag fits over the back of the front seat of the car. Its different-sized pockets can accommodate any number of things, but it's especially good for children's clutter that accumulates in the car. Small toys, crayons, bottles, and books fit nicely in this organizer, keeping the car neater and serving as an entertainment center for the children when they are riding in the car.

CAR VISOR VALET — This organizer clips onto the visor to hold a map, pen, sunglasses, and other critical clutter. Simple yet effective, it can put the essentials within easy reach at all times.

CLOSET SYSTEMS — There are all kinds of closet systems, from wood to wire, from double-hang-instant-install to custom-built. This is not one product, but a variety of products and services. They may feature shelves, drawers, cubbyholes, pull-out bins, and accessory organizers like shoe, belt, and tie racks.

COAT TREE — This oldie but goodie is still the answer for people who have limited coat closet space. Placed by the entry, it holds coats and hats on hooks — even the children can master the art of hanging up their coats on a coat tree.

DISH CADDIES — These quilted plastic covers are designed to hold dishes so that they can be stored. The extra protection offered by the covering's thickness keeps the dishes clean and helps eliminate the chipping that results when dishes are bumped up against each other. Generally, good sets of china (rather than everyday dishes) are stored in these covers.

DISHPAN — Rubber dishpans can hold anything that will fit into them, from toys to tools to car cleaning supplies. Label the dishpan to indicate the contents and store it on a shelf or in a cabinet. You can even put a toddler's socks in one, and put it on her closet floor. Dishpans last just about forever, and their potential use is unlimited.

FOLDING CRATE — This crate, made of heavy-duty plastic, is the size of a small box and can hold anything a small box can. It is especially good for transporting items, since once you have used it, it can be folded flat for storage. Keep it in your car trunk and use it to move groceries or children's car clutter. It can also contain the car safety equipment in one concentrated area of the trunk, eliminating those rolling thumps you hear from time to time as the extra can of oil slides around the trunk.

FOOT LOCKER — Foot lockers will hold just about anything you want them to, but because they are so durable and relatively inexpensive, they can be put to use most effectively in the basement or garage to hold some of the clutter that might be stored in those areas. Poisonous gardening supplies can be locked into the trunk away from children's curious fingers, or you can use the foot locker to store your out-of-season ski gear. Used by military personnel worldwide, the foot locker can stand years of abuse while it stores your gear in that hinterland known as the garage or basement.

GIFT WRAP ORGANIZER — This organizer, generally made of heavy-duty cardboard material, organizes several rolls of gift wrapping paper, ribbons, and other miscellaneous gift wrap clutter. The whole thing can be stored in a closet or in a work area next to a table, ready for you to wrap the next last-minute gift with creativity.

HAT BOXES — Hat boxes are back in vogue, and can be stacked and used to store hats. Often attractive, they can also be put on a shelf to hold other items, such as memorabilia or small craft supplies. A large hat box can even provide a little girl with the perfect container for her dollie's clothes.

KEY CLAMP — Key clamps enable you to clamp your keys to the strap of your handbag (either to hang outside the bag, or tuck inside, as you like) or onto belt loops. Men have known about these for years, and people who use a lot of keys find the key clamp is a lifesaver. This clamp is available at locksmith shops.

KITCHEN CENTER — A free-standing kitchen center can house extra appliances, bulky pots and pans, and a microwave oven. Some centers have extra power outlets so that you can operate the appliances right on the center, freeing up otherwise cluttered kitchen counter space. Still other centers have a butcher block top to give you extra food preparation space. Most move on wheels and are easy to incorporate into the average kitchen, providing extra functional space without the cost of custom cabinetry work.

KITTY LITTER PAN — Use this for lots of things other than kitty litter. Tools, cassette tapes, sewing patterns, and toddler's books (placed standing up) can all be put in a kitty litter pan to be stored on a shelf, in a cabinet, or under the bed. You can use it to store art supplies or coloring books and crayons. When it's time to work on that next project, just carry the pan, with all of the colorful supplies in it, to the work area. Cleanup is easier than before, since it's simple for everyone (especially children) to put everything back in the pan for storage until needed again.

LAUNDRY BASKET — Laundry baskets can hold laundry, balls, out-of-season blankets, toys, and folded gift boxes. Keep a laundry basket handy, and when the children destroy a room with toy clutter, you can facilitate the cleanup by tossing everything into the basket, where it can be tucked temporarily in a corner or carried to the bedrooms for redistribution of the toys.

LAZY SUSAN TURNTABLES — These are made of plastic or rubber and come in all sizes, with some available stacked one on top of the other, double-decker style. Use these to hold cosmetics, vitamins, spices, teas, small jars of food in the refrigerator, and some craft and sewing supplies. Under the sink, bathroom or cleaning supplies can be placed on a large, sturdy Lazy Susan. When you want something, you don't have to reach to the back of the cabinet, knocking down all the cans and bottles in front.

LID STORAGE RACK — These can be placed inside a cabinet or on a shelf near the cooking area to hold lids for your pots and pans. Some lid racks can attach to the inside of a pantry door to hold a few lids (but only if you have clearance between the door and the shelf). These racks cut down on the clanging and aggravation that goes along with locating the right lid for the pot that you are using.

LINGERIE BOX — Made of plastic, these boxes are usually transparent and have tops that can be white, pink, blue, or transparent. They fit easily on a shelf, or under the bed, and can be used to store not only lingerie, but out-of-season things like gloves and long johns. Love letters, memorabilia, and photos can also be stored and stacked neatly in these boxes. Cassette tapes, scarves, and small stationery supplies can also be housed in these boxes. Their transparency and stackability make them a storage solution for clutter problem areas in every room of the house.

METAL PARTS CABINET—These cabinets come in different sizes and feature a series of small drawers that are perfect for holding hardware, stamps, game parts, and assorted gadgets, doodads, and gizmos that need to be organized to avoid having that all encompassing "junk drawer" spread to other drawers in the house, basement, or garage.

MUG RACK—Made of wood, this expandable peg system holds not only mugs on the kitchen wall, but is perfect for hats, scarves, handbags, and necklaces. It can be hung on the back of the closet door, on the kitchen wall, in the entry, or in your dressing area or bathroom to keep things stored yet instantly accessible.

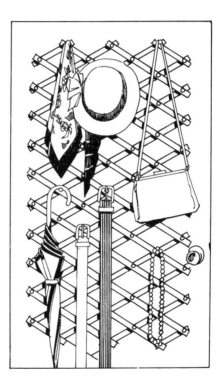

OVER-THE-DOOR RACK—These coated wire racks fit nicely over a door—usually the pantry—to hold cleaning supplies and/or canned goods. You can also mount some of them directly onto the basement or garage wall to help organize small cans of paint and jars of nuts and bolts and other miscellaneous supplies. If you're especially short on bathroom space, you can put one of these on the back of the bathroom door to hold your bathroom supplies—from witch hazel to hair spray. It's the quickest way to provide substantial extra storage space for any canned or bottled goods.

ROLLING BASKET SYSTEM—Without the butcher block top, these rolling baskets can be adapted to hold all baskets, or to handle file folders and baskets. The cart is suitable for storing underwear in your closet, linens such as placemats and napkins, produce such as potatoes and onions, paper bags, gift wrapping paper and ribbons, craft and art supplies, or sewing supplies. By incorporating file folders with the baskets, you can have a cart that stores special projects in progress, household accounts and incoming mail, and children's school papers and art projects. As clutter containers go, this cart is one of the most versatile organizers you can use. Its convertability guarantees that you can use it for years to come. When the children leave home, you can move it to the kitchen or your closet. When you take up embroidery, you can use it as a storage cart that can be wheeled to your work area (your easy chair). When you're done with that special charity project that is generating so much paperwork, the basket can give you extra storage in your closet for scarves, stockings, and sleepwear. This clutter container will adapt to your changing needs.

SEWING BASKET — These baskets are organized specifically to hold sewing supplies, particularly threads, needles, and bobbins. Some sewing baskets are actually baskets, while others are made with quilted material and are shaped like small cases. Organizing sewing supplies into one of these can make getting ready to sew an uncomplicated process, with the supplies logically arranged for your sewing needs.

SHELF DIVIDER — These plastic or wire dividers clamp onto a shelf and provide a vertical divider point wherever they are placed. These are handy in a closet shelf where sweaters or T-shirts are stored. The dividers keep the stacks neater and help prevent collapsing piles. They can also be used in some linen closets to separate pillowcases, tablecloths, placemats, and sheets. With the shelf divider, even if one pile collapses on you, your chances are excellent that the other stacks will stay neatly in place.

SHOE BAGS — Shoe bags can be hung in a closet or on the back of a bedroom or closet door to hold shoes. This is a good alternative to putting shoes in a jumble on the closet floor; it keeps the shoes clean and organized, making dressing and closet organization easier to deal with.

SHOE RACKS — Shoe racks are made to either sit directly on the closet floor or to hang over the back of a closet or bedroom door. Like shoe bags, the shoe rack will keep your shoes organized for easy selection. Since there is nothing covering the shoe at all (like the bag portion of the shoe bags), you can find the shoes you need at a glance.

SHOE STACKER — This shelf system is placed directly on the closet floor and shoes are set onto the shelves, organized by pairs. You can use it on the closet floor for shoes or, in the winter, you can put it in the entry so that wet shoes and boots can be temporarily stacked for drying and access when you need to go out again.

SPICE RACKS — These racks come in all sizes and are made in wood, plastic, and wire materials. They can be mounted on the wall to keep spices within easy reach.

SPORTS GEAR RACK — This wire organizer can hold a small selection of sports gear, including baseball bats, hats and the like.

It can be mounted on any wall, and because it is relatively contained, can be a good solution for people without garage or basement space to accommodate sporting equipment. This rack can go inside a hall closet to help you get your gear up and out of the way while making it easily accessible.

STAIRSTEP SHELVES — These shelves can add to a cupboard's efficiency by making it possible to put containers (such as spices and cooking items or canned goods) into the cupboard in a staggered manner. This makes it easy to see what is behind the items in the front of the cupboard, and helps eliminate knocking over cans and bottles in the front to get to the items in the back.

STOCKING BAG — This hanging bag holds several pair of stockings in vinyl see-through pockets, making it easy to ascertain what stockings you have on hand so you can select what you need for the day or make a note to stock up on others. For people short on drawer space, a stocking bag, hung either inside the closet or on the closet door, can be a helpful storage solution.

STRIP RACK — These simple clamp strips can be mounted on a wall or inside a utility closet to hold brooms, mops, and the like on the wall, with the clamp action keeping the item affixed to the wall. Heavy-duty strip racks can be installed in the basement or garage to hold outdoor gear like shovels, rakes, and brooms. Inside or outside, strip racks can organize items that might otherwise end up in a jumble somewhere, or worse, misplaced or lost because there was no special place to store them.

SUPPLY CADDY — This inexpensive organizer not only holds but transports things that could otherwise turn into clutter. Originally meant to hold cleaning supplies (which can then be carried from room to room when cleaning), this caddy can also be used to hold some small art and craft supplies, as well as office

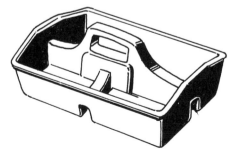

supplies such as pens and pencils, paper clips, and rubber bands. This container can also handle a few small tools or miscellaneous hardware. Made of durable, easy-to-clean plastic, the caddy holds several items in one place and can be easily carried to the project at hand.

SWEATER BOX — This clear plastic box with cover is similar to a lingerie box but is deeper, and provides excellent storage for a multitude of items other than sweaters. Two or three years' worth of bank statements fit easily into one sweater box, and larger photographs also fit easily into the box. Assorted memorabilia, special linens, fabric and patterns, love letters, and craft supplies can all be stored in these boxes, which can then be stacked in a cabinet or closet, or stored under the bed. It's a snap to see what is in the box. Since they're so easy to stack, you can triple the storage space available to you on a top closet shelf by using these boxes rather than large cardboard boxes or piles stacked directly onto the shelf itself.

TACKLE BOX — Metal or heavy-duty plastic tackle boxes feature trays that can hold any small items that could benefit from organization by category. Nuts, bolts, and screws, along with a few small tools, can be stored in a tackle box. Some art, crafts, and sewing supplies, along with children's marbles, cosmetics, or small hair accessories, might also do well in a tackle box. Sales people who work from the car can turn a tackle box into a portable desk by using it to store pens, pencils, paper clips, rubber bands, stapler, etc. Tackle boxes provide creative storage for small clutter and can be carried from place to place.

TIE RACK — Tie racks come in all shapes, sizes, and styles, and are made primarily to hold ties. But some tie racks can do double duty by providing the necessary hooks to hang and organize belts, and some lightweight handbags. Women can also use them for their "ties" — those small silk ties that are tied in a bow with suits. A tie rack can also hold hair ribbons or strips of finishing fabric, like lace. Whatever the tie rack is used for, it can be an effective solution for organizing items that would ordinarily get tangled and/or wrinkled when you're not wearing them.

TOOL BOX — Tool boxes are most effective when used for tool storage, but can be used to hold other items that might be carried from place to place. In the car, a tool box can hold flares and other safety supplies, or it can store crayons and other small toys to keep the children occupied when they are in the car. Art and craft supplies, and traveling office supplies can be stored in these boxes and carried to the work area as needed. It makes containing and moving lots of small things easy.

TOY CAGE — A toy cage is a coated wire crate on wheels that is a simple solution to moving and/or picking up toy clutter from room to room. Toys, balls, or stuffed animals can be stored in this box on wheels and can be pulled from room to room, depending on the play area of the moment. The open design makes it easy to see what's inside the cage without dumping everything out, and even if everything is dumped out the child can toss it all back into the cage and pull it back to where it belongs.

TRANSFILE BOXES — These sturdy boxes are sold in stationery and office supply stores unassembled (flat). They are easy to store and easy to assemble. You can use them for papers, files, documents, car supplies (those kept in the trunk), or miscellaneous canning supplies, for example. Regardless of where you buy them, the boxes are uniform in size, making them easy to stack. The handles on the boxes also make them much easier to move.

TRASH CANS — Trash cans of all sizes can be used to store items like balls, sporting equipment (such as bats), rolled-up art, and large rolls of wrapping paper.

TRUNKS — Trunks are good for storing everything from blankets to memorabilia. Wicker, antique wood, and cedar trunks can also often be turned into a small table by putting a piece of glass over the top of them. (See also FOOT LOCKERS.)

UNDERBED STORAGE DRAWER — These pull-out or roll-out storage drawers make storing things under the bed convenient and dust-free. Blankets, linens for the bed, out-of-season clothes, and games can all be stored under the bed in these drawers. Shoes and socks for small tots can be put in these drawers to help facilitate dressing in the morning, since children often hate the idea of closets. You can store family records or photo albums in these drawers, or, if you want to keep letter-writing materials near the bed where you work on such projects, you can keep some of those materials in the drawers, along with a magazine or two to keep you busy enough to fall asleep productively.

UNDERSINK ROLL-OUT BASKETS — These two-tiered wire basket systems mount on rollers in a cabinet so that you can pull the basket out for easy access. Generally these are used to hold cleaning supplies, and make pulling out what you want very easy, eliminating the problem that arises when you need to get something in the back of the cabinet and can't do it without knocking down the cans and bottles in the front. Besides kitchen use, these can be mounted under some bathroom sinks to hold extra bathroom gear, and this too can be helpful in storing supplies, particularly cleaning supplies.

UTENSIL RACK — A utensil rack is designed to hold the utensils that you use most often in the kitchen—spatula, large spoons, etc. It might also be adapted to hold necklaces or ribbons, as well as some craft supplies (such as embroidery hoops). Utensil racks can be mounted onto the wall, or can be purchased as a free-standing unit and kept on the counter near the stove. If you use it for another purpose, keep it on a table, shelf, or dresser top.

WRAPRACK™ — This rack holds and dispenses paper towels, tin foil and food wrap, and can be mounted on the wall or on a cabinet door. It organizes wraps that might otherwise get crammed into an available drawer, and puts them within easy reach when you need them.

© Atlantic Representations, Inc.

ZIP-LOCK BAGS — These bags can be purchased at the grocery store and can be a good see-through container for things such as game pieces, craft parts, makeup, or small fabric scraps.

Recycling Your Clutter Cast-Offs

It should be easy for you to weed out some of the clutter you never use when you stop to consider that there are other people less fortunate than you who could use those things every day, starting today. If you're at a loss as to who to call for your giveaways, use these charities as your starting point: Salvation Army, Missions for the Homeless, Veterans' Charities, Battered Women & Abused Children's Charities, Senior Citizens' Facilities, Goodwill, Catholic Charities (check with your local parish), Local Churches, Medical Charities (such as Hospice groups).

Here are some other, more specific, giveaway ideas:

ANTIQUES AND COLLECTIBLES — If you have items of value, such as antiques or collectibles, that you are willing to part with, talk to an auctioneer about selling these items for you. As long as you are willing to ask a low enough consignment price to allow a reasonable profit for the auctioneer and a good selling price to the buyer, he or she should be able to sell the goods for you.

BOOKS — Once you finally bite the bullet and decide to get rid of some of those millions of books you have all over the place, the easiest and by far the nicest thing to do is to call your local library to see if they would like a donation. (They won't take outdated reference books, however.) You could also donate the books to your local secondhand bookstore. If it just about kills you to "donate" to a profit-making organization such as a secondhand bookstore, ask the proprietor to give you ten cents per book. If they agree, take the money and run. And remember: Nobody, but nobody, wants those bazillion copies of *National Geographic* that you are warehousing.

HOLIDAY CARDS — If you've collected Christmas cards, you can now cheerfully send them to the St. Jude's Ranch for Children, a home for abused and unwanted children. The children use the cards to make new holiday cards by cutting the pictures off the used ones and gluing them onto new backing. The school sells the final product and uses the funds to help with their operating costs. Send used Christmas cards *only* to: St. Jude's Ranch for Children, P.O. Box 985, Boulder City, Nevada 89005.

JUNK MAIL — Although no charity wants your junk mail, there is a way to get rid of most of it. You can stop it before it even starts. Write to the Direct Mail Marketing Association and tell them you want the junk mail stopped. They will arrange to stop your name from being sold to most large mailing-list companies, which should reduce your junk mail influx substantially. Just think of all the trees and personal time you will save by heading off all that junk mail at the pass. Write to: Mail Preference Service, Direct Mail Marketing Association, 6 East 43rd Street, New York, New York 10017.

JUNK AND TREASURES — Bearing in mind that one person's junk is another's treasure, you can plan a garage sale. Be sure to get an early start, post lots of signs, and display your treasures and junk as attractively as possible. You'll sell everything from old underwear to furniture as long as you remember that people are looking for bargains. If you want good or even fair prices, forget the garage sale and rent a storefront. Think of the garage sale this way: It's a great way to have other people actually pay you to haul this stuff off. At the end of the day, you can deliver what is left to your local charity (do NOT put it back into the house), or you can park it at the curb with a huge FREE sign on it. What a way to go.

NEWSPAPERS AND MAGAZINES — Although many recycling centers won't take old magazines, they will take newspapers. Check with your local recycling center to see if they take magazines and find out where you can drop off your recyclable paper. Then, if you don't have time to deliver those stacks of paper, hire a teenager who drives to do it for you.

OLD EYEGLASSES — If you have old prescription eyeglasses, you can send them to New Eyes for the Needy. This charity sells metal glass frames to a refiner and uses the funds to purchase new glasses for the needy. Other types of framed glasses in good condition are sent to third-world countries for use by the needy there. Send your glasses to: New Eyes for the Needy, 549 Millburn Avenue, Short Hills, New Jersey 07078.

Resource Helpline

These resources provide services and products that can help you conquer (and store) your clutter:

ACME DISPLAY FIXTURE CO.
1057 S. Olive Street
Los Angeles, CA 90015
(213) 749-9191

San Diego: (619) 236-9114
San Francisco: (415) 392-1818

Hangers and closet fixtures at wholesale prices (call for catalog).

BED, BATH & BEYOND
715 Morris Avenue
Springfield, NJ 07081
(201) 379-4203

(Over 30 locations; call for location nearest you)
Home and closet organizing products and systems.

CALIFORNIA CLOSET CO.
6409 Independence Avenue
Woodland Hills, CA 91367
(818) 888-5888

(Over ninety locations; call for location nearest you)
Custom closet design and installation.

CLOSET FACTORY
(Corporate Offices)
12800 S. Broadway
Los Angeles, CA 90061
(213) 516-7000

(Several locations nationwide; call for location nearest you)
Custom closet design and installation.

CLOSET MAID
Clairson International
720 W. 17th Street
Ocala, FL 32674
1-800-221-0641
1-800-421-0104 (in Florida)

Closet and storage systems and accessories.

THE ORGANIZATION
Stephanie Culp
P.O. Box 890700
Temecula, CA 92589-0700
(909) 506-0044

Professional organizer, author, and speaker on organization and time management.

DAY-TIMERS, INC.
Allentown, PA 18001
(Send for catalog of products)
(215) 395-5884

Personal planning systems and office products.

DAY RUNNER, INC.
2562 Eastham Drive
Culver City, CA 90232
1-800-232-9786
1-800-635-5544

Personal planning systems and related products.

EQUIPTO
225 S. Highland Avenue
Aurora, IL 60507
(312) 859-1000
1-800-323-0801

All steel shelving, racks, drawers, and bins for workshops.

HOLD EVERYTHING
Williams Sonoma
Catalog Mail Order Department
P.O. Box 7807
San Francisco, CA 94120-7807
(415) 421-4242

Catalog.

KARTELL U.S.A., INC.
P.O. Box 1177
Greenville, SC 29602
1-800-845-2517

Storage furniture, accessories.

MESSIES ANONYMOUS
5025 S.W. 114 Avenue
Miami, FL 33165
(305) 271-8404

Education for Messies: seminars, newsletters, books, and self-help groups.

LEE ROWAN
Consumer Affairs
6333 Etzel Avenue
St. Louis, MO 63133
1-800-325-6150

Home and closet organizing products.

RUBBERMAID, INC.
Consumer Services
1147 Akron Road
Wooster, OH 44691

Household organizing products.

SHURGARD SELF-STORAGE CENTERS
(175 locations in the U.S.; check your local directory)

Self-storage units; packing supplies.

TECHLINE
Marshall Erdman & Associates
5117 University Avenue
P.O. Box 5249
Madison, WI 53705
(608) 238-0211

Wall units and storage furniture.

LILLIAN VERNON
510 S. Fulton Avenue
Mount Vernon, NY 10550
(914) 633-6400

Catalog.

WE'RE ORGANIZED LTD.
1050 W. Central
Brea, CA 92621
1-800-826-9590

Modular garage storage systems.

About the Author

Organization and time management expert Stephanie Culp is the author of several books, including *How to Get Organized When You Don't Have the Time, Conquering the Paper Pile-Up, Organized Closets and Storage for Every Room in the House*, and *Streamlining Your Life*. Her organization and management consulting firm, The Organization, designs and implements systems and establishes procedures to help businesses and people get, and stay, organized so that they can benefit from maximum personal power and professional productivity.

Culp is a national lecturer and seminar leader specializing in time and paper management. Her articles have appeared in several publications, including *The Los Angeles Times, Redbook, Working Woman, Family Circle*, and *Milwaukee Magazine*.

She was elected as a delegate from Southern California to the White House Conference on Small Business in Washington, D.C. in 1986. She is a founding member and the past president of the National Association of Professional Organizers; she has received that association's award for her outstanding contribution to the profession three times and is the only professional organizer to hold that distinction.

Stephanie Culp designs and implements systems and establishes procedures to help businesses and people get, and stay, organized. If you, your group, or company would like to have Stephanie help you get organized or serve as a speaker or trainer, you may contact her directly at:

Stephanie Culp
the Organization
P.O. Box 890700
Temecula, CA 92589-0700

(909) 506-0044
(909) 506-0024 (fax)

Get the Most Out of Life

with help from organization experts Stephanie Culp and Don Aslett!

Stephanie Culp's 12-Month Organizer and Project Planner— This is the get-it-done planner! If you have projects you're burning to start or yearning to finish, you'll zoom toward accomplishment by using these forms, "To-Do" lists, checklists and calendars. *#70274/$12.99/192 pages/paperback*

How to Get Organized When You Don't Have the Time—You keep meaning to organize the closet and clean out the garage, but who has the time? Stephanie Culp combines proven time-management principles with practical ideas to help you clean up key trouble spots in a hurry. *#01354/$12.99/216 pages/paperback*

Lose 200 LBS. This Weekend—Experience the freedom of having a clutter-free house, mind, and body! Don Aslett's motivational guidance and practical organizational advice is fun and inspiring, packed with quick tips and easy solutions you can apply to your daily life immediately. *#70504/$12.99/160 pages/paperback*

No Time to Clean—Spend more of your precious time doing the things you enjoy! Inside you'll learn how to clean faster and more efficiently, reduce clutter and messes, make cleaning last longer, and set cleaning schedules that work with a hectic lifestyle. *#70505/$12.99/192 pages/paperback*